13/299

AFTER THE EXILE

A Pocket Guide to Haggai, Zechariah and Malachi

CONTENTS

INTRODUCTION

The final three prophetic books of the Old Testament were all written after the terrible experience of God's people in exile in Babylon. They were written by godly men who sought to bring God's word and direction to a group of people who were seeking not only to rebuild Jerusalem but their lives as well.

So much had changed in the lives of the Jewish people over the preceding 70 years. Most will have been born in the time of exile from the Promised Land. The oldest had experienced the trauma of the destruction of Jerusalem and being carried onto captivity by the Babylonians. Now they faced the challenge of being God's people in a time of change and challenge.

Each of the prophets has their own distinctive style and message. Where there are overlapping themes, it is because God was wanting to emphasise important principles to His often wayward people.

Whilst these messages from God were written or proclaimed to a particular people in a particular time and for a particular purpose, we should not dismiss them as being irrelevant to us in our times. God's Word is timeless and the principles of scripture can be applied in every age. God Himself does not change. This powerful truth is recorded by Malachi (3:6).

This book is an introduction to the three prophets and their messages. It is not a full commentary to the Biblical books but, I hope, a practical tool to begin to get to grips with their contents. It can be usefully used by both individuals and small study groups. The discussion questions are designed to stretch our thinking and help us to engage more fully with reading the text.

I hope that this pocket guide will encourage you to dig deeper into God's Word and find your faith challenged and growing.

David Chapman

Yaxley 2020

HAGGAI

HAGGAI
INTRODUCTION
Who was the author and when was it written?

Little is known about the prophet Haggai except what is found in the book that bears his name. Ezra mentions him briefly in association with the prophet Zechariah and the rebuilding of the temple (see Ezra 5:1; 6:14). The name Haggai means *"festival"*, an appropriate meaning given the prophet's work in restoring temple worship. What is most remarkable about Haggai's ministry is perhaps its brevity; his messages were given in only four months in 520 BC.

Haggai was a prophet to the Jews who had returned from the Exile in Babylon. His first task was to force them to see where their hearts and priorities really lay. He urged them to do what they should have done from the start: to rebuild the temple with a willing heart. To these admonitions he added the promise that God would be with them. With this promise, the people could return to their first enthusiasm and carry out God's purposes for them. Then their worship would be joyful and sincere.

Haggai was a contemporary of Zechariah and as such he was one of only three post-exilic prophets, the third being Malachi.

Historical Setting

When some of the Israelites returned from the Babylonian captivity beginning in 538 BC, they determined to restore the worship of God to its rightful place at the centre of their lives. They planned to build a new temple in Jerusalem (see Ezra 1). Sadly, however, their resolve seems to have vanished shortly after their arrival in Jerusalem. They built an altar on the original temple site and later laid the foundations for the new temple. But when enemies who lived in the area applied pressure, the Persian king ordered the work on the temple to cease. A later king of Persia, Darius I, lifted the restrictions that had been placed on the rebuilding of the temple and told them to proceed. However, even when the barriers were lifted, the people lapsed into spiritual lethargy. They were not the idolaters that their ancestors had been, but they had lost their early passion for the worship of the living God. They explained their behaviour by advancing the time-honoured excuse of procrastination: it just does not seem to be the right time (see 1:2).

When Haggai confronted the people, he addressed the problems of his day: the infertility of the land and the tough economic times (1:6). But he did not blame these problems on poor planning. Instead, he urged the people to focus on their spiritual condition. They were focusing on insignificant matters like the decoration of their homes, while every day they ignored God's temple which was lying in ruins. The temple was more than a building. It was the site where the people met with the living God. It was the symbol of the abiding presence of the Creator of the universe. If the people ignored the physical ruin of the temple, they were also ignoring the spiritual wreckage in their souls as well.

Zerubbabel the governor and Joshua the high priest, together with the people of God, responded swiftly to the message (1:12). Three weeks after Haggai gave his first message, they began their work on the temple. Anticipating a positive response, Haggai came with another message. This was a simple one, but it had profound implications: Haggai assured them that the Lord was with them (1:13). This was the same message that Moses had brought to the Israelites in Egypt (see Exodus 3:8). Indeed, this would be the name of the coming Messiah — Immanuel, God with us (see Isaiah 7:14). When the people chose to make God the centre of their lives, the Lord would Himself remain in their midst even without a physical building.

TIMELINE

539 Babylon is overthrown by Cyrus (Persian)

538 Cyrus issues a decree allowing the exiles to return

536 Temple construction begins

530 Temple construction halted

520 Temple work resumes

516 Temple completed

Key verses

- 1:4
- 2:6 -9
- 2:15 – 19

OUTLINE

The Lord's first message: Consider your ways

1:1 – 15

What you have done – neglected God's house (1-6)

What you should do – build God's house (7 – 11)

Results of considering your ways (12 – 15)

The Lord's second message: Be strong and work 2:1 – 9

Comparison of the new temple with Solomon's temple (1 – 3)

A call to be strong (4 – 5)

Coming glory of the new temple (6 – 9)

The Lord's third message: I will bless you

2:10 23

A question for the priests (10 – 19)

A promise for Zerubbabel (20 – 23)

The message for today

We need to ensure that our priorities are right in God's sight.

If God gives you a task do not be afraid to start it.

The Holy Spirit is with us in our work for God.

Be an encourager!

Theology of the book

To emphasize some key points about the people's attitude towards God, Haggai posed a couple of questions. One of these was about the laws concerning what was clean and unclean (2:10–14). These laws had several purposes:

(1) they protected people from diseases

(2) they taught certain spiritual lessons

(3) they created in the people an instinctive sense of right and wrong

In other words, they underscored the message that the Lord, and not any person, determines what is good or evil. Haggai asked the priests if cleanness or holiness might be transmitted through touch. The priests answered that it could not. Then the prophet asked if uncleanness could be transmitted through touch. The answer was yes. Haggai applied this principle to the nation. An indifferent attitude toward the construction of the temple had polluted everything the people touched. Their attitude made the work of their hands unacceptable to the Lord. Even though the temple work had begun, the people's hearts left them unclean in the eyes of the Lord. Nevertheless, God, in His great grace, would still bless His people.

In a question and answer format (2:15–19), Haggai also encouraged the people to think about their circumstances before they started to build the temple. None of their past work had resulted in success: *"Is the seed still in the barn?"* (2:19). But from that day onwards God would bless His people because they had reordered their priorities. They had put the worship of the Lord before their own welfare (1:4, 14). Out of the bounty that the Lord would provide, the Israelites would be able to bring the proper sacrifices of true worship into the new temple.

Questions to think about and discuss

1. Before studying Haggai now, what did you know about the book?

2. How important do you think the context of the message is to the message itself?

<u>CHAPTER ONE</u>

What you have done – neglected God's house (1-6)

The book begins by accurately dating when the message from Haggai was given. The prophet spoke to the people over a period of just four months in 520 BC. His message came to two important people, Zerubbabel who was the governor of Jerusalem and Joshua who was the High Priest. We can perhaps see here a combination of the prophetic, political and priestly coming together to see that God's will is done in the lives of His people.

Haggai begins by bringing the word of God to His people. He describes God as the Lord of hosts (the Lord Almighty). He uses this description of God fourteen times in this short book. Haggai is emphasising the power and majesty of God. To a dispirited people this was a way to encourage them to look up from their troubling, anxious circumstances and look to their mighty God.

Haggai's first word to the people is challenging. He has heard from God and what God is saying about His people is that they believed that the time was not right to build the house of the Lord, the Temple. Their priorities at this time lay elsewhere.

In verse 3 Haggai speaks and accuses the people of being so concerned with their own wellbeing and comfort that God's work and Temple were being neglected. He contrasts the new splendour of their wood panelled houses with the dereliction of God's house.

Haggai says that God is calling on them to *"Consider their ways"*, to think about what they are doing and what is going on around them. In verse 6 God says that they are using their comparative material poverty as an excuse for neglecting the Temple. It seems that no matter what they did they saw little fruit or benefit from it. Their materialism has not brought satisfaction to them and now was the time for them to see that their approach to life, and in particular their neglecting of God, resulted in a barren experience. In fact, because of their self-reliance and self-indulgence God had allowed their society to be unfruitful (see verse 9).

What you should do – build God's house (7 – 11)

In verse 7, for a second time, God calls on His people to *"consider your ways"*. He urges them to go up to the surrounding mountains to gather wood to be used in the Temple rebuilding project. Evidently there was sufficient material to complete the task but it needed people to go and bring the wood. Of course, this would take effort. The trees need to be felled, stripped and transported from the mountains into Jerusalem.

God was quite happy for them to use the natural, common trees of the local area for the rebuilding. Remember that the original Temple had been built with beautiful cedar wood transported from Lebanon and with costly gold brought from Ophir. God was more interested in the hearts and motives of the people than the costliness or beauty of what they built.

From verses 9 to 11 we learn that their lack of material prosperity was as a result of God's actions. Because His house, the Temple, was still in ruins He had withheld His favour from them. The earth would not produce the crops they needed. God had called a drought over the land which blighted the production of grain, olive oil and wine. Even people and livestock were affected by His actions. The natural world is affected by God's actions, His judgement. Within His creation it is only mankind that is disobedient to His commands.

Results of considering your ways (12 – 15)

The response of both of the leaders, Zerubbabel and Joshua, together with the people is encouraging. Verse 12 says that all of them obeyed the voice of the Lord and the prophetic words spoken by Haggai. There was a recognition that the Lord had sent Haggai, that he was a true prophet of God. Not only did they obey the voice of the Lord and the words spoken by Haggai but we are told that *"the people feared the presence of the Lord".* From a position of paying lip-service to God they had been brought to a place of fearing the Lord. They had recognised that as Haggai brought His Word it was as if the Lord was in their midst.

God recognised their change of heart and attitude and He spoke through Haggai a word of encouragement in verse 13, *"I am with you".* What a wonderful thing it is to know that God is with us and not against us. We should note that as soon as the people obediently responded to God's prophetic word, He drew close to them.

We are told in verse 14 that the Lord stirred up the spirits of Zerubbabel, Joshua and all of the remnant of the people. From a position in which the people of Jerusalem had been facing the wrath of God due to their disobedience now He was acting in their lives. The result of God's action was that they resumed the rebuilding of the Temple. When God stirs someone's spirit it should result in action. We might perhaps think of the time recorded in Acts chapter 2 when God sent the Holy Spirit to the disciples in Jerusalem. The waiting believers were empowered by God to go and preach the gospel, not just have a praise party.

In the final verse of the chapter, once again, we see the author precisely timing when these things happened. It was on the twenty-fourth day of the sixth month, in the second year of King Darius' rule. Haggai had begun to prophesy on the first day of that month and now the people were responding with actions in obedience to God's commands and wishes.

Questions to think about and discuss

1. How do you think this chapter shows the consequences of disobedience to God?

2. If God were to speak to you today as He did to Haggai in verses 2 and 3 what would he say it is time for in your life?

3. What are God's people challenged to do in this chapter?

4. From what we see in this chapter God could clearly exercise His anger against disobedience. How should this fact affect the way we seek to serve God today?

CHAPTER TWO

Comparison of the new temple with Solomon's temple (1 – 3)

Nearly a month passes until Haggai prophesies again. On the twenty-first day of the seventh month he begins to speak. Once again, he is called by God to speak to Zerubbabel, Joshua and the remnant.

The work had been going on to rebuild the Temple but it appears that the enthusiasm for the work is beginning to flag. Haggai challenges the people to press on with the task.

Some of those who had returned to Jerusalem from exile had, in their childhood or youth, seen Solomon's Temple in all its glory before the Babylonian army destroyed it. Haggai speaks directly to these people in verse 3.

Compared to Solomon's Temple the building that was being erected seemed *"as nothing"*. It is easy to understand why some of these people would be adversely affected by comparing the two buildings. Doubtless some of them would be speaking out their thoughts and this would discourage those who were actively involved in the construction works.

A call to be strong (4 – 5)

Faced with the pessimism that was spreading among the people Haggai addresses himself to the ruler, Zerubbabel, the High Priest, Joshua and the people as a whole. His message from God is clear to all of them, *"Stay strong!"*. God says, firstly in verse 4, that He is with them, they are not alone in the task before them.

In verse 5 God reminds them of the covenant He had made with them when He brought them out of Egypt. He says that His Spirit remains with them. In fact, God had never fully forsaken His people despite their sin and disobedience. Yes, He had chastised and disciplined them but He had never deserted them.

As well as calling them to stay strong God also commands them *"do not fear!"*. It is not clear why the people might be fearful but we can perhaps assume that they nervously looked around Jerusalem and saw potential enemies encircling them. They had benefitted from the Persian ruler's favour when he agreed to let them return to Jerusalem. Another ruler might change that policy. A jealous enemy who saw a new Temple built in Jerusalem might take action to ensure the Jewish people remained subdued. We may recall the opposition that Nehemiah faced approximately 100 hundred years later when he rebuilt the walls of Jerusalem despite being sent by the ruler of the Persian Empire.

In every age believers need to heed the call of God to both stay strong and to not fear. The promises that God made to the people in Jerusalem through Haggai apply to us too. God is with us; His Spirit remains with us. We do not look back to the same covenant that they had with God but instead look to the better covenant sealed by the shed blood of Jesus at the Cross.

The coming glory of the new temple (6 – 9)

As the people looked at the emerging Temple it would have been difficult for them to envisage it as being a building of glory. Haggai speaks the word of the Lord in verse 6 where God declares that He would shake heaven and earth, the sea and the dry land. Most commentators would see this as a prophecy that has not been finally fulfilled. There have been many times throughout history when it seems that God may be shaking the earth, however, all of these have been partial.

In its immediate context it is likely that God is referring to the rising power of Alexander the Great of Greece who would defeat the Persians. The balance of political and military power would swing from Persia towards European powers, Greece and subsequently Rome.

The final consummation of the prophecy will be when Jesus returns *("the desire of nations")*. In Hebrews 12:26 – 27 we see these verses referring to Jesus' return and the shaking of all nations at that time. With Jesus' return the land will finally have the promised eternal peace that so many have desired to see.

We may perhaps see in these verses a hint of the judgements to come that are recorded in the book of Revelation.

The people are defiled (10 – 14)

Just over two months later Haggai again has a message from the Lord for His people. Haggai has two questions for the priests. There answers would then be linked to God's message to the people. In Leviticus 10:10 one of the tasks of Aaron and his descendants was to judge whether a thing is clean or unclean.

At first sight the two questions appear to be concerning the Law as it relates to clean and unclean items and so the priests are the people who should know and be able to give sound judgements. Questions such as these were often debated by the scribes and priests as they sought to understand the Law. In Jesus' day the scribes and priests has codified the Law into far more clauses than Moses ever gave to the people. Their interpretations were given as much weight in many peoples' minds as the Scripture themselves.

In Haggai's exchange with the priests we can perhaps hear echoes of Jesus' discussions with the scribes and the Pharisees.

Firstly, Haggai asks the priests whether a piece of consecrated meat that has been carried in a garment would make that garment or anything the garment touches also consecrated. The priests reply *"no"*. They do not elaborate on their answer. According to Leviticus 6:27 the garment would be declared holy but the things that the garment touches will not.

Secondly, Haggai asks the priests whether, if a person who has become defiled by touching a corpse then touches the same things as the garment mentioned in the first question, would those things also become defiled. Again, the priests are quick to answer *"yes, they would become defiled".* In Numbers 19:11 – 13, 22 we see the principle that anything that touches something that is defiled becomes itself unclean.

Both questions revolve around the possibility of whether something can transmit holiness or uncleanness to something else. It seems that ceremonial uncleanness is much more easily transmitted than holiness.

Was God simply using Haggai to examine the priests as to whether they knew the letter of the Law? No, He had a bigger purpose than that in mind. In verses 14 God applies the principles to His people. God sees them as a people who have become defiled and so any items that they touch also become defiled.

Simply being back in the Promised Land from exile did not mean that they automatically became a holy people. In order for them to be seen by God as a holy people they needed to behave and live as a holy people. This involved obedience to God's statutes and guidance. This was a huge challenge to a people who had lived amongst pagan people and who had little personal experience of God and His blessings.

A promise of blessing (15 – 19)

Having brought these challenging questions Haggai then brings an encouraging message from God.

God calls His people to *"give careful thought"* to their position. He repeats this command three times in these few verses. Whenever a challenge from God comes it serves us well to ponder and meditate on it before rushing on with our lives.

God encourages them to look back and see how tough their situations had been, principally economically, before they began to rebuild the Temple. They would recall that there was never the quantity of supplies that they had anticipated. God says that the poor harvests they had experienced were a direct consequence of their sinfulness. He had struck the crops with blight, mildew and hail (see v 17).

Before the Israelites entered the Promised Land God had set before them both blessings and curses, The Land could have been *"flowing with milk and honey"*, the blessings of obedience or it would be filled with thorns and difficulties which were the curses of disobedience. These consequences were clearly set out by Moses as recorded in Deuteronomy chapter 28.

God then says that from this particular day, the twenty fourth day of the ninth month, His blessing would begin to be upon them. He is very particular in His promise to them. Up to that time their crops had produced nothing but from that day He would bless their harvest. His promise was related to a number of different types of produce. He mentions seed, fig trees, vines, pomegranates and olives. In future days they could look back to see when God began to bless them.

This promise of blessing is intrinsically linked to their obedience in rebuilding the Temple. Before they rebuilt there was curse upon the land but now, as they begin to rebuild a Temple for His glory, God says that a promise of blessing would be upon the land.

The choosing of Zerubbabel (20 – 23)

On the same day, the word of the Lord came again to Haggai. On this occasion, rather than being a message for all of the people, the message is for Zerubbabel who was the Governor of Judah.

Zerubbabel faced a difficult task. He not only had to try to lead the people of Judah he also had to ensure that he was obedient to the King of Persia. He would also need to be able to negotiate with the neighbouring peoples who were often hostile towards the Jews in Jerusalem and Judah.

The message for Zerubbabel begins with a warning, a repetition of verse 6. A time of shaking is coming upon the earth and the heavens. Those who trusted in political or military power will be overthrown. The imagery is violent and vivid. In verses 22 and 23 the words translated as *"overturn"* and *"overthrow"* are the same as used to describe the destruction of Sodom and Gomorrah (see Genesis 19:25 and Amos 4:11). The mention of overthrowing chariots and riders would remind Zerubbabel of the destruction of Pharaoh's army at the Red Sea (see Exodus 15). The reference to armies fighting amongst themselves echoes the story of the destruction of the Midianites in the time of Gideon (see Judges 7:22).

With these prophecies of destruction Zerubbabel could be forgiven for feeling nervous. How would he and the people he was responsible for cope with the coming pressures and dangers?

God speaks directly to him to reassure him. In the days when the world is shaken God assures him that He has chosen Zerubbabel. This should strengthen him for whatever tasks he has to deal with. In fact, God says that He would use Zerubbabel like a signet ring (v 23). A signet ring would be given by a ruler to a representative or ambassador who can act on behalf of the ruler. The ring would signify the authority of the representative to deal on the ruler's behalf. The use of the ring would guarantee that whatever is pledged by the representative would be fulfilled by the ruler.

Prior to the exile in Babylon the prophet Jeremiah had brought a message to King Jehoiachin that if the king were God's signet ring then God would pull off the ring and hand the king over to Nebuchadnezzar (see Jeremiah 22:24). Now God is promising Zerubbabel that He would use him. In these final verses God specifically refers to Zerubbabel by name to reassure him of the favour that God had placed over his life.

With this final word of comfort Haggai's brief period as a prophet to the nation comes to an end. We know nothing more about Haggai's life subsequent to this period. Nevertheless, his obedience to God in speaking words of challenge and comfort is a great example to us.

Questions to think about and discuss

1. How does God encourage His people in this chapter?

2. What promises does God make to His people in this chapter?

3. What lessons can you learn and apply to your own life from reading this chapter?

ZECHARIAH

ZECHARIAH

Who was the author?

Zechariah's father, Berechiah, probably died when his son was young, making Zechariah the immediate successor of his grandfather, Iddo (Nehemiah 12:4). Iddo was a priest who returned from Babylon with Zerubbabel and Joshua and was, according to tradition, a member of the Great Synagogue (the governing body of the Jews before the establishment of the Sanhedrin). Zechariah, then, was a member of the tribe of Levi and probably served as both a priest and as a prophet. He entered his prophetic ministry two months after his contemporary Haggai had concluded his first oracle Haggai (Ezra 5:1; 6:14).

The name Zechariah is a common one in the Old Testament. In fact, there are 27 other people who share the same name. The name means "*Yahweh remembers*".

There are those who question the unity and single authorship of Zechariah. They usually believe that chapters 9 to 14 date from the Hellenistic period (331–167 BC) or the Maccabean period (167–73 BC). The reference to *"Greece"* in 9:13 has sometimes been cited as evidence for a late date, after Alexander's conquests (c. 330 BC). However, Greek influence was strong in the ancient Middle East as early as the seventh century BC. Greece is mentioned by the eighth century prophet Isaiah (see Isaiah 66:19, where Greece is referred to as Javan) and the sixth century prophet Ezekiel (see Ezekiel 27:13, 19 for Javan). Those who hold to the unity of the book generally date its completion between 520 and 500 BC.

Zechariah began his prophetic ministry in the second year of the Persian king Darius (522–486 BC) and his last dated prophecy was delivered two years later, in 518 BC.

Historical Setting

Zechariah lived and prophesied during the period in Israelite history following the Babylonian captivity (597–538 BC). The great prophet Jeremiah had predicted that the Israelites would return to the Promised Land after seventy years of discipline in exile. God began fulfilling this promise when He raised up Cyrus, King of Persia, whose military exploits brought about the capture of Babylon in 539 BC. Following his victory, Cyrus decreed that all exiled peoples could return to their homelands.

The people of Judah were among those who benefited from this reversal of Babylonian policy. More than 50,000 Jews returned to Palestine from Babylon in 538 BC. The first group of Jews returned under the leadership of Sheshbazzar, prince of Judah (Ezra 1:8) in 537 BC. The altar for the temple was erected in the autumn of that year, but construction of the temple itself did not begin until the spring of 536 BC. They laid the foundation of the Temple in 536 but opposition stalled the work for about 15 years (Ezra 1:1-4; 4:1-5). Darius Hystaspes (1:1), who came to the throne in 521, confirmed Cyrus's decree, and Zechariah, like Haggai, encouraged the people to finish the Temple (which they did in 516 BC).

During the sixteen years of neglect the people of Judah lost their vision and sense of spiritual purpose. Their procrastination resulted in divine chastening (Haggai 1:11; 2:17). Although the crops failed and the people languished, they still did not repent until God raised up two prophets to turn the people back to Himself. In 520 BC, Haggai called for the Israelites to recognize their spiritual priorities and rebuild the temple. Zechariah began his prophetic ministry just two months after Haggai (compare 1:1 with Haggai 1:1).

The ministries of Haggai and Zechariah did not cease when work began in earnest on the temple. The prophets continued to encourage the people. Haggai's messages were delivered in 520 BC; Zechariah's last dated prophecy was given in 518 BC (7:1). With the people committed to restoring the worship of the Lord and the Temple, God poured out His blessing on a repentant and spiritually revitalized people. The Temple was completed in 515 BC and rededicated with great rejoicing.

What are the purpose and themes of the book?

Zechariah's prophecies had two purposes.

Firstly, they challenged the returning exiles to turn to the Lord, to be cleansed from their sins and to experience once again the Lord's blessing (see 1:3).

Secondly, Zechariah's words comforted and encouraged the people regarding the rebuilding of the temple and God's future work among His people (1:16, 17; 2:12; 3:2; 4:9; 6:14, 15).

In the first chapters, Zechariah encourages the people by focusing on God's choice of Jerusalem (1:17; 2:12; 3:2). The Lord had not abandoned His ancient covenant people. Through Zechariah, God not only reaffirmed Jerusalem's divine election, but promised to come among His returning people and live in their midst (see 2:10, 11; 8:3, 23). It was through His **personal** presence among His people that God would accomplish a miraculous work.

In the second half of the book, Zechariah details God's future dealings with His chosen people. He reveals the eventual defeat or overthrowal of all of Israel's enemies. He prophesies concerning the future glories of Zion and the universal reign of the Messiah. This is perhaps the overarching theme of the book: the complete restoration of God's people would occur through the redeeming and delivering work of the coming Messiah.

Theology of the book

Zechariah teaches a great deal concerning the First and Second Comings of Jesus the Messiah.

He refers to the Messiah as:

- the *"branch"* (3:8)

- God's *"Servant"* (3:8)

- God's *"Shepherd"* (13:7)

There is also an allusion to the Messiah's ministry as a Priest-King in 6:13 (see Hebrews 6:20–7:1).

Furthermore, Zechariah prophesied:

- the Messiah's entrance into Jerusalem on a colt (9:9; see Matthew 21:4–5; John 12:14–16

- His betrayal for thirty pieces of silver (11:12, 13; see Matthew 27:9, 10)

- the piercing of His hands and feet (12:10; see John 19:37)

- the cleansing from sin provided by His death (13:1; see John 1:29; Titus 3:5).

Of all the prophetic books Zechariah, principally chapters 9 to 14, is the most quoted section of the Prophets that can be found in the New Testament Gospels.

Concerning the Messiah's Second Coming, Zechariah prophesied such future events as:

- the conversion of Israel (12:10 – 13:1,9; see Romans 11:26)

- the destruction of Israel's enemies (14:3, 12–15; see Revelation 19:11–16)

- the reign of Christ in a New Jerusalem (14:9, 16; see Revelation 20:4–6).

Together with his emphasis on the Messiah, Zechariah also has an important message about God's plan for salvation. The importance of repentance and returning to the Lord is emphasized in the introduction (1:3–6). In 3:1–5, Zechariah provides a striking illustration of the removal of sin and the imputation of righteousness. The removal of the high priest's filthy garments and the provision of clean robes illustrates the work of Christ. Through His atoning death, Christ cleanses us of our filthy sins and clothes us with His own righteousness. It is only in this way that we can approach a holy God and be found to be acceptable to Him.

Genuine religion, according to Zechariah, is not found in external acts of religious piety, but instead it is based upon a personal relationship with God (7:5–7). Such a relationship with God should also change attitudes to neighbours. Like the prophets before him, Zechariah condemned the oppression of the widow, the orphan, the stranger and the poor (7:10). As a preacher of righteousness, he called God's people back to the virtues of justice, kindness, compassion and truth (7:9; 8:16).

Key Verses

4:6 – depend on the Holy Spirit to accomplish all that God calls you to do

8:16, 17 – be honest, truthful and act with integrity and justice in your dealings with other

12:10 – a clear prophecy concerning the sufferings of Jesus

OUTLINE

Zechariah is a book of consolation and hope. It begins with a call to repentance and concludes with prophecies concerning the future return and reign of Christ. The book offers spiritual strength, encouragement and motivation. For a people who were discouraged, struggling and tempted to quit this book helped them to pick up the pieces and press on with God.

I   The call to repentance 1:1-6

II. The visions of Zechariah 1:7-6:15

    A. The Horses and Riders 1:7-17

    B. The Four Horns and Four Craftsmen 1:18-21

    C. The Surveyor 2:1-13

    D. Joshua the High Priest 3:1-10

    E. The Golden Lampstand 4:1-14

    F. The Flying Scroll 5:1-4

    G. The Woman in the Ephah (basket) 5:5-11

    H. The Four Chariots, 6:1-8

    I. The Crowning of Joshua, 6:9-15

III. Questions concerning fasts 7:1-8:23

A. The Fasts 7:1-3

B. The Failure of the People 7:4-14

C. The Future for Jerusalem 8:1-23

IV. Prophecies (oracles) concerning the future 9:1-14:21

A. The First Prophecy 9:1-11:17

1. The victories of Alexander the Great 9:1-8

2. The comings of the King 9:9-10

3. The victories of the Maccabees 9:11-17

4. The blessings from Messiah 10:1-12

5. The rejection of the Shepherd 11:1-17

B. The Second Prophecy 12:1-14:21

1. The Lord's care for Jerusalem 12:1-14

2. The Lord's cleansing of Jerusalem 13:1-9

3. The Lord's Second Coming to Jerusalem 14:1-21

Questions to think about and discuss

1. Before beginning a closer look at Zechariah, how would you summarize what you already know about the book?

2. If you are already familiar with this book which passages are your favourite parts of it?

3. From what you see in the words of the Lord in 1:3, what would be a good personal prayer to offer to God as you study this book?

CHAPTER 1

Opening verses

The opening verses of the prophecy set the scene for the reader. The date that the prophecies were given and details of who the prophet was are made clear.

The initial prophecy is given in the eighth month of the second year of King Darius' reign. This dates it at 520 BC. The prophet is identified as being the grandson of Iddo who himself had been a prophet. He also belongs to a priestly family.

He prophesies at a similar time to Haggai. This is a period when God was calling the people of Jerusalem to rebuild the Temple following their return from exile in Babylon. Unlike Haggai who mainly urges the people to rebuild, Zechariah also calls them to repent and return to the Lord. He takes restoration to another level by calling the people to a covenant renewal alongside their rebuilding project.

The call to repentance (1 – 6)

Zechariah reminds his hearers of the punishment that God had inflicted on their rebellious forefathers. The majesty and power of God is emphasised in that he uses the term *"Lord of Hosts"* 53 times during the book. Their God is the Lord of the armies of the universe, both spiritual and material.

He calls them to return to God with the promise that if they do so then God would also return to them. There are echoes of both Isaiah's and Jeremiah's words prior to the Exile in Babylon (see for instance Jeremiah 3:12).

He reminds them that the prophecies that God had sent them prior to the Exile had all come true. The words that God had given to them had *"overtaken"* them and they had justly suffered the consequences of their disobedience.

The vision of the horses and riders (7 – 17)

Three months after calling the people to repentance Zechariah receives his first vision. It is the first of a number of night visions that come to him.

In his first vision Zechariah sees a man on a red horse standing among myrtle trees in a hollow. Behind him are other horses, red, sorrel and white in colour. Although it does not say that there are riders on the other horses the likelihood is that there are (see v10).

The horses are in a camouflaged setting (the myrtle is a bush that grows to between 6 to 8 feet high) and in a hollow, ravine or in the shadows. In other words, they are not clearly seen from a distance.

There are two angels identified in the passage, these are the *"angel who talked with me"* and the *"Angel of the Lord"*. The two angels are working together to provide revelation. Zechariah asks the subordinate angel a question (v9) and this angel takes him to his commander (the Angel of the Lord, *"the man on the red horse"*) who provides the answer.

The vision is explained as being a picture of a force sent out by God to reconnoitre the world. The report from the reconnaissance party is that the earth is currently resting at peace (11). This apparently hopeful report is soon overturned as the Angel of the Lord cries out to God, rather like a prophet, *"How long?"*

The Angel of the Lord does not want peace on the earth, instead he wants there to be an upheaval that will see God's people arise to their rightful place in the earth. He recognises that God has been angry with

His people for 70 years, surely now was the time for mercy and restoration.

God replies to the Angel with *"good and comforting words"* (v 13). There is an echo perhaps here of Isaiah 40:1 – 2.

The Angel commands Zechariah to proclaim God's message. In verses 14 – 17 he is to announce salvation to the people of God. The message is highly emotional, flowing from God's characteristic zeal for His people. God's passion for His people is reflected at times in his care for them, but when they do not display exclusive devotion to Him then He is passionately jealous for such devotion.

In this prophecy God's zeal for His people is also linked to His anger towards the nations surrounding His people, those who had abused them. The anger towards His people is less than the level of abuse inflicted on them by those nations.

In verse 16 the Lord declares that He is returning to His people in Jerusalem in mercy. He is looking towards the completion of the rebuilding of His Temple in Jerusalem. The surveyor's line used in building will be stretched out not only over the Temple but over the whole city. God is concerned for the whole of His people's lives not just the *"religious"* part. This picture echoes some of the imagery of Ezekiel (see Ezekiel 43:4 and 40:1 – 3).

In verse 17 God expands the picture of healthy restoration as He declares that prosperity will spread out across the land and that He will again choose to bless Jerusalem.

The vision of the four horns and four craftsmen (18 - 21)

Zechariah now recounts a further vision, this time of horns and craftsmen. It is likely that the horns can be identified as representing the Babylonians and also the Assyrians (who took God's people, Judah, Israel and Jerusalem, into exile) and the craftsmen or ploughmen as representing the Persians (who overthrew the Babylonians and allowed God's people to return from exile). In the Bible horns often represented the strength of an army. It represents an aggressive weapon. The picture is of a de-horning taking place across the world (in the four corners of the earth).

Historically around this time some provinces of Persia had rebelled against King Darius and supported a man called Gaumata. These rebels had come from the

Babylonian provinces and they were totally destroyed.

The imagery is of animal horns that scattered God's people which are then in turn seen off (terrified) by craftsmen or labourers. God's people had been so downtrodden that they could not even lift their heads (v21). Now those who had been their oppressors would be thrown off and sent on their way by a stronger force.

This scene is one that should bring hope to God's people. They will not be oppressed forever. The Assyrians and Babylonians will no longer hold power over the Jews because the Persians have arisen as a benevolent servant in the hands of God. The punishment of Babylon provides comfort and hope to a discouraged people.

Questions to think about and discuss

1. In verses 1 – 6 what would you say are:

      The brightest promises

      The most fearful warning

      The most urgent command

      The most painful accusation

2. In simple terms how would you explain the two visions in verses 7 to 21?

The vision of the horses and riders

The vision of the horns and the craftsmen

CHAPTER 2

The vision of the surveyor

Zechariah sees a vision of a man with a measuring line. When questioned the man tells Zechariah that he is measuring Jerusalem. The angel who was with Zechariah meets a second angel who tells him that one day Jerusalem will outgrow its current dimensions. They would expand beyond their protective walls. This prophecy is similar to Jeremiah's earlier prophecy given in Jeremiah 31:38 – 40. God promises that when they expand beyond the walls, He would guard them Himself, He would be their wall of protection. It is possible that this prophecy may have been intended to encourage other Jews to return from Babylon who perhaps had been fearful about their safety. Some had preferred to remain in Babylon where they had become prosperous and felt more secure there than in a city that was only gradually being rebuilt following its destruction.

God further encourages the exiles to return in verses 6 & 7. There is the threat to the Persian rulers of Babylon that God would move against them. Those Israelites wo remained in Babylon and shared the decadent lifestyles of the Babylonians would suffer along with them when God acted. Sadly, many Jews chose to remain away from Jerusalem and were subsequently scattered.

In verses 8 to 13 God speaks words of warnings to the Gentile nations who might seek to harm His people. In verse 8 He describes Israel as His *"prized possession"* or the *"apple of His eye"*. The *"apple"* is a description of the iris which is the most sensitive part of an eye. If anything touches the iris the eyelid automatically closes in protection. God warns that anyone who attacks His people will have to deal with Him. Perhaps as Christians we need to remember what Jesus said in Matthew 25:34 – 46 in the parable of the sheep and goats, "*as much as you have done it to the least of these my brethren, you do it to me.*" We must ensure that we do not treat fellow believers unkindly or with contempt. God sees what we do and regards our actions towards others as if we were acting towards Him.

After issuing a warning to those who would harm His people God then promises that nations will join themselves to Him (see verse 11). God is the universal God not just Israel's God. We can remember His promise to Abraham in Genesis 12:3, *"All the families on earth will be blessed through you."* This promise is fulfilled through the coming of Jesus the Messiah. Since His coming people from many nations have been enabled to come to God through Him. We who are New Testament Gentile believers have been grafted into the olive tree of God's Promise (Romans 11:17 – 24).

God's final command in this chapter is for all of mankind to be still before God. He has roused Himself and we must stand back and see what He will do. In God's presence we should have a great sense of awe, respect and wonder. Simply being quiet is not enough, we humbly bow before the great and mighty God of all Creation.

Questions to think about and discuss

1. Why do you think that the city would have no walls? What is the significance of it?

2. Why did God want His people to flee?

3. How attached are we to the world? Are we in danger of not hearing God's call to flee from it (see 1 John 2:15)?

CHAPTER 3

The vision of Joshua the High Priest

Joshua (or Jeshua) was the High Priest when the remnant returned to Jerusalem and began the task of rebuilding the city and Temple (see Haggai 1:1).

In this vision Zechariah sees Joshua being accused by Satan (the Accuser). In the vision Joshua stands as a representative of the nation. We do not know exactly what Satan accused Joshua of but we can deduce from God's response that he was accusing Joshua of being unworthy and unrighteous. God rebukes Satan and declares that He chose and chooses His people in spite of their sin. Satan is continually accusing God's people (see Job 1:6). However, he greatly misunderstands the breadth and depth of God's mercy and forgiveness toward those who believe in Him.

In verses 2-4 the vision graphically shows how we receive God's mercy. We can do nothing ourselves. God removes our filthy clothes (our sins) and provides us with fine, new clothes which represent the righteousness and holiness of God (see 2 Corinthians 5:21, Ephesians 4:24 and Revelation 19:8). Joshua is pictured as being plucked from a destroying fire. This is a powerful picture of how God rescues us.

In verses 5 – 7 God speaks directly to Joshua. He emphasises the need for Joshua to obey Him and walk in His ways. If he does so, he will then have delegated authority from God over the Temple. Remember that in Exile there had been no functioning priesthood, it needed to be reinstated when they returned from Exile.

In verses 8 & 9 God reminds Joshua and the other priests that their ministry would one day cease, they were symbolic of something greater that was to come. What was to come was the Branch, the Messiah (see also Isaiah 4:2 and Jeremiah 23:5).

The meaning of the seven-sided jewel is obscure. We do not know what will be inscribed by God on the jewel. Seven sides may indicate perfection of beauty. What is perhaps clear is that God promises to remove their sins in a single day (see 1 Peter3:18).

Verse 10 is a picture of a future time of peace when neighbours would share together under their vine. This is a picture of security and provision. In ancient Israel this was a picture of the good life. It was their idea of heaven on earth and therefore spoke of abundant blessing.

Questions to think about and discuss

1. How would you explain the meaning and significance of this vision to a new believer?

2. How would you respond to Satan if he accused you of sinning?

CHAPTER 4

The vision of the golden lampstand

Zechariah is awoken once again by the angel and sees another vision, this time of a golden lampstand flanked by olive trees. The angel explains the meaning of the vision to Zechariah.

In verses 1 – 5 the gold lampstand with a bowl and seven lamps on it represents a steady supply of oil. This signifies that God's power would be reflected in the light. The oil was obtained from crushed olives and used in bowls with wicks to produce light. In the Bible oil is often a symbol of the Holy Spirit.

In verses 6 & 7 Zechariah is given a message for Zerubbabel, the governor of Jerusalem. Zerubbabel had been given the responsibility of rebuilding the Temple (see Ezra 3:2,8 and Haggai 1:1). While the prophets encouraged the people to build. it was his responsibility to see it through to completion. He is reminded that all will be accomplished by relying on God's Spirit and not on human ingenuity or strength. It is only through God's Spirit that anything of lasting value is accomplished.

The people who had returned from exile may have been weak, harassed by enemies, tired and discouraged but they had God on their side. The picture of Zerubbabel placing the capstone of the Temple displays an extraordinary show of strength (like Samson in Judges 16:3).

In verses 8 – 10 another message comes for Zerubbabel. God declares that he will complete the task he began. There were some who had returned from Babylon who had seen Solomon's Temple in their youth. When they looked at the smaller Temple being built, they were disappointed. God encourages Zerubbabel not to despise a day of small things because He was rejoicing in what was being done. As an aside we are told that the seven lamps represent God seeing everything happening on earth.

In verses 11 – 14 Zechariah asks the angel to explain what the olive trees and branches represent. He is told that they represent two heavenly beings who stand in the court of the Lord. Sadly, we can only speculate as to who they are. Some commentators believe that they are Joshua and Zerubbabel. Others believe there may be a link to the two witnesses who are found in Revelation 11:3 prophesying to the nations during the Great Tribulation.

This seems perhaps unlikely as neither Joshua nor Zerubbabel were prophets.

Questions to think about and discuss

1. How would you explain the meaning and significance of the visions in the last 3 chapters?

2. How would you restate in your own words God's message to Zerubbabel in 4:6?

CHAPTER 5

The vision of the flying scroll (1 – 4)

Zechariah now sees a scroll flying through the air. The scroll is large measuring approximately 30 feet by 15 feet. The length would not be extraordinary in those times but generally a scroll would be a maximum of 1 foot in width. Rather than being held in someone's hands the scroll is suspended in the air. The size of the scroll means that the message can be spread quickly and over a large area.

There is writing on both sides of the scroll announcing God's curse on those who steal and those who blaspheme or swear falsely by His name. This may remind us of Exodus 32:15 where we are told that the tablets of the Law were written on both sides. Both of the sins mentioned are contained in the Ten Commandments given by God to Moses. One relates to man's relationship to God and the other to man's relationship to their neighbours. God is warning His people that He continues to be committed to the covenant principles outlined in the Mosaic law.

The vision of the woman in the basket (*Ephah*) (5 – 11)

This vision proceeds through three stages:

1. The prophet sees a measuring basket which is then interpreted by the angel (5,6)

2. A lead cover is raised to reveal a woman who is then identified (7,8)

3. Two winged women appear and their significance is revealed (9-11)

The measuring basket (ephah) is flying through the air. There is a divergence amongst commentators as to what the basket represents. This is partly due to differing translations. The NIV, which follows the Septuagint, says that the basket represents the iniquity of the people. The NKJV (which follows the Hebrew text and Latin Vulgate) says that it represents *"their resemblance throughout the earth"*. The problem is due to one disputed consonant – *"ynm"* or *"wnm"* in the scripts. The following parts of the vision fit the NIV (*"iniquity"*) more readily.

The content of the basket is revealed to be a woman covered by a lead disc. The disc is used to keep the woman from escaping from the basket. The angel says that the woman represents Wickedness. The basket will eventually be taken to Shinar (Babylon). It is likely that the representation of wickedness as a woman reflects the prevalence of idolatrous worship of female deities (e.g. Asherah, Ishtar, Astarte). The term used for wickedness is often used in the Old Testament to describe the idolatry of the nations surrounding Israel.

The prophet then sees two women with powerful wings come and lift up the basket to take it away. The wings are said to be like those of a stork. Under the law the stork is an unclean creature (Leviticus 11:11) and so may be an appropriate creature to carry away a basket full of wickedness to an idolatrous destination. It is perhaps interesting that rather than calling the destination Babylon the word Shinar is used. Shinar is the area that contains Babylon and is where the Tower of Babel was constructed, an attempt by humanity to invade God's realm. The basket will come to rest on a *"house"* or *"temple"* constructed specifically for it.

Questions to think about and discuss

1. In verse 3 which land did God curse and why?

2. Why have a lead cover on a basket?

3. Why set the basket down in Babylon?

CHAPTER 6

The vision of the four chariots (1 – 8)

Zechariah now sees a vision concerning four chariots pulled by horses which are differently coloured. When he enquires as to what they are he is told that they were spirits of heaven that go out to do God's will, often to bring His judgment. We note that they are also similar to the horses found in Revelation 6:1 – 8. There, the red horse represents war, the black horse represents famine, the white represents victory and the dappled represents plagues or disease.

God commands them to go out over the earth, each in a different direction. The red's direction is not mentioned but we can perhaps assume it is going east as that direction is not mentioned. Alternatively, it may mean that God is holding some judgment in reserve.

The chariots are similar to what Zechariah saw in his first vision. In verse 8 Zechariah is told to note that the mission sent to the north has been completed, God's wrath has been vented on it. The north would, perhaps, represent Babylon.

The crowning of Joshua (9 – 15)

Zechariah receives instructions from God. Men would come from Babylon with silver and gold. Zechariah is to make the silver and gold into a crown. This crown will be for Joshua the son of the High Priest Jehozadak. There would then be a coronation in the Temple.

It would be unusual to see a priest crowned as crowns are generally associated with kings. As Joshua is a priest he cannot be from David's line (Jewish priests are Levites not Judahites). Their Persian masters would be pacified because they would see a priest-king as less of a threat than a political or military king. Note that the last time that it is recorded that Jerusalem had a priest-king it was Melchizedek (see Genesis 14, Hebrews 7).

There are promises of expansion attached to Joshua who is referred to as the Branch. This word has previously been used as a reference to the Messiah (see Isaiah 11:1-3, Jeremiah 23:5-6). It is likely that the Messianic fulfilment of this prophecy began to be fulfilled when Jesus came and will be fully completed at His Second Coming.

The Crown was to be kept in the Temple because the Messiah would be both King and Priest ruling from the Temple. The purpose was to also remind the priests of the coming role that the Messiah would play. They could then expect and anticipate His coming.

In verse 15 there is mention of people coming from afar to Jerusalem. The near fulfilment of this would be the continuing return from the Babylonian exile, the distant fulfilment will be when the Gentiles flock to Jerusalem to *"build"* the Messiah's Temple.

Questions to think about and discuss

1. How would you explain the meaning and significance of the visions in this chapter?

2. What harmony is meant in verse 13?

3. Look carefully at the Lord's words in 6:9 -15. What exactly does He tell Zechariah to do and for what purpose?

CHAPTER 7

Obedience is better than fasting (1 – 7)

The next two chapters date from roughly two years after the series of visions that Zechariah had previously received.

The first word from the Lord concerned fasting. Depending on the translation either men had come from Bethel, which had formerly been a religious centre in idolatrous Israel, to the *"house of God"* (i.e. the Temple in Jerusalem) or they had come from elsewhere, perhaps as exiles, to the Temple.t

They asked if they should continue to fast in the fifth month as they had done throughout the time of Exile. This fast was to commemorate the fall of Jerusalem and the destruction of the Temple in the fifth month 587 BC (2 Kings 25:8 – 12, Jeremiah 52:12-16). They asked the question to the priests and to the prophets, the two sources of revelation in the Temple precincts.

The answer that comes from the Lord is a challenge to those who heard it. They were challenged as to the integrity of their fasting, were they really fasting unto the

Lord? There is a questioning of their motives and attitudes, both in times of fasting and feasting. Obedience to God's word brought by the former prophets (such as Jeremiah) would have meant that the fasting in exile would not have been necessary. This thought leads naturally to the next section.

Disobedience resulted in captivity (8 – 14)

In 8 – 10 Zechariah brings a message that could have easily come from the mouths of Jeremiah, Isaiah or Amos. He brings 3 exhortations and 2 prohibitions as he challenges his hearers.

They are encouraged to:

- Execute true justice (not just the letter of the law)
- Show mercy
- Show compassion

They are prohibited from:

- Oppressing widows, orphans, aliens or the poor
- Plotting evil in their hearts against a brother

There is nothing new here apart from the fact that it is only here in the Old

Testament that you find all four categories of vulnerable people mentioned together.

Zechariah reminds his hearers that their forefathers had disobeyed God's commands and exhortations in the past. They had hardened their heart and stopped up their ears. The consequence of this was that God had ignored their cries when they came and His wrath had fallen upon His people. God had scattered them among the nations. The pleasant and fruitful promised land had become desolate. The inference is that the current generation needed to heed the lessons their ancestors had failed to learn.

The challenges to the generation described by Zechariah are challenges we may face today. He calls us to listen to God and change our ways.

Questions to think about and discuss

1. We are now halfway through Zechariah's prophetic book. How would you summarise what the most important things that have been taught so far are?

2. What is the most urgent command that you see in this chapter?

3. What is the most important aspect of God's character that is revealed in this chapter?

CHAPTER 8

God's salvation of the remnant (1 – 13)

In this section we find a number of short messages or oracles. Each of them is prefaced with the words *"This is what the Lord Almighty says".*

1. God declares how jealous or zealous He is for Zion.

2. God's presence would return to Jerusalem. This would transform its status to become the City of truth, the Holy Mountain.

3. A picture of renewed prosperity and security. The vulnerable young and old will be at rest and at play.

4. The people may marvel at the changes coming to Jerusalem but they will not surprise God. He is central to the transformation.

5. God will bring His scattered people back to Jerusalem and they would once again be His people.

6. There are contrasts between the former curse and the future blessings promised by God. God promises the resources to rebuild the Temple and

the city's economy. The land will now be blessed because of God.

God's new determination (14 – 15)

This short section refers back to issues mentioned in chapter seven. Here we find once again mention of God's anger towards those of His people who had disobeyed Him in the past. Now there is a new determination on God's part to bless His people. The use of the word *"determined"* emphasises God's intentions. Zechariah ends this section with the familiar words *"do not be afraid"*. To a remnant who are still suffering the aftereffects of God's discipline these will have been comforting words.

God's ethical demands (16 – 17)

Having encouraged His people that He would bless them, God then outlines some of His ethical demands. They are familiar commands:

- Speak truthfully to one another
- Practice truth, justice and peace in their legal system (*"in the gates"*)
- Do not harbour evil intentions towards others
- Do not swear falsely

It is precisely these things that God had complained of regarding their ancestors. God uses emotional language concerning the two prohibitions, He declares that He *"hates"* those things.

Transforming fasts to feasts (18 – 19)

The next word from God partially refers back to the question raised in chapter 7 regarding fasts. God says that all of the fasts practiced by the Jews in exile will be transformed into times of festival or celebration. They had not been wrong to fast during their exile but now a new era was beginning in their relationships together and with their God. At the end of verse 19 there is again a reminder that they needed to love truth and peace if they expected to see this new era continuing into the future.

Impact on the nations – (20 – 23)

The final two oracles of the chapter concern the future.

The first reflects a strong tradition in the prophets in which nations are drawn to Jerusalem to seek God (see especially Isaiah 2:2-4 and Micah 4:1-5). It is not only the scattered remnants of Israel who will come to Jerusalem but Gentile nations too.

The second oracle builds on the first (*"in those days"*). When the nations begin to come up to Jerusalem the Jewish people will play their part. People will want to accompany the Jews to Jerusalem because they have heard that *"God is with them"*. The obedience of the Jews will usher in a new era in which Jerusalem will fulfil its original purpose as the place of God's manifest presence on earth. This prophecy is almost certainly related to the End Times.

Questions to think about and discuss

1. From this chapter what do you think God wants us to understand about His plans and purposes for His people?

2. Imagine that God wanted to highlight some things from this chapter for your life. Which verses would He highlight?

CHAPTER 9

God returns in triumph (1 – 8)

Chapter 9 is an oracle (prophecy) of the future. It describes the triumphant return of God to Zion. The oracle begins with a depiction of God as a warrior marching from north to south defeating Israel's traditional enemies (Syria and Phoenicia in the north, the Philistines in the south) before returning to His temple in Jerusalem.

God's actions would see the political power of Damascus (Syria) broken and the financial power of Tyre destroyed.

Traditionally, Tyre was a powerful stronghold that had held out against the Assyrians for five years (ending 622 BC) and against the Babylonians for thirteen years (ending 572 BC). Later, Alexander the Great would capture the city but he only achieved this conquest by building a causeway to reach the island. Tyre was renowned as a rich merchant city; it was full of wealth. This prophecy says that God would destroy both the city and its wealth.

The destruction of Tyre would send shockwaves down the coast to the ancient Philistine cities of Ashkelon, Gaza, Ekron and Ashdod. In Zechariah's day these towns were densely populated and were under Persian rule. Nevertheless, they were still seen as symbols of Israel's enemies and a threat to the realization of God's promise to the people of Israel. These towns would be stripped of population (Ashkelon), pride (Ashdod) and leadership (Gaza). God would deal with their pagan rituals and sacrificial practices.

The second part of verse 7 has a surprising twist. It reveals that God's purpose is not only to cleanse the land but also to create a remnant of Philistines who would serve Him. This remnant from Ekron (the closest Philistine city to Judah) are compared to the Jebusites who were destined for destruction (Exodus 23:23) but were instead integrated into the Israelite community (Joshua 15:63, 2 Samuel 24:16 – 25). In this prophecy the Ekronite community will not be treated as second-class citizens but will even be honoured as leaders in Judah.

In verse 8 the divine warrior reaches His destination at the temple in Jerusalem. He will encamp against marauding enemy forces. Consequently, there would not be a return to the conditions of the Babylonian Exile. God would be watching over His people.

The king receives His kingdom (9 – 10)

Having returned to Jerusalem in the first section of chapter 9 God now proclaims the coming of a king for Jerusalem. The king is depicted as a humble figure (*"gentle"* in the NIV). The term used was often used of the poor and needy in society. This king enters the city not on a stately horse or chariot (symbolic of military power and success) but on a lowly donkey. The verse perhaps looks back to Jacob's prophecy concerning Judah (Genesis 49:10 -11).

In verse 10 warfare weapons are removed (chariot, horse, battle bow). Without the use of these weapons the king will still exercise a peaceful rule not only over Judah but to the ends of the earth.

These verses are seen as partially fulfilled when Jesus rode into Jerusalem on Palm Sunday but will be fully fulfilled on His Return (see Matthew 21:1 – 11).

The people return to the kingdom (11 – 17)

On the basis of the blood covenant that He has made with the people of Jerusalem, God promises salvation for his people. The mention of the blood covenant is perhaps reminiscent of Exodus 24:8 where the covenant was ratified after the reading of the Law by the sprinkling of blood on the people. The mention of being freed from a waterless pit may remind the Israelites of the story of Joseph (Genesis 37:24, 39:20,22).

Both Judah and Ephraim are said to be used by God as battle weapons (13). These two tribes are often seen as the main representatives of the Israelite tribes (Judah in the south and Ephraim in the north). The prophecy perhaps looks forward to a restoration of the united kingdom of Israel (as in David's day).

The reference to *"sons of Greece"* is perplexing. Some see it as having been added later after Alexander the Great's era. However, during this period of Persian rule they were already warring against Greece. In that case mention of Greece may not be anomalous. The word translated as Greece is *"Javan"*. In the tables of the nations in Genesis 10 Javan is a son of Noah's son Japheth.

In verse 14 the image changes to a battle scene. The divine warrior is likened to an approaching storm. Lightning is seen as God's arrow and thunder as God's trumpet. Protected by God, His people gain victory not with sophisticated weapons but with slingshots. There are echoes here of David's victory over Goliath in 1 Samuel 17. The second part of verse 15 describes the victory in battle through powerful imagery of wine and sacrifice.

Verse 16 begins with a summary of what God has done for His people; He has saved them. The familiar imagery of God's people as His flock and He as their shepherd is used. They are also called sparkling jewels of a crown (see also Isaiah 62:3). They will experience blessed provision in their new land.

Questions to think about and discuss

1. Look again at verse 9. As a prophetic passage about the coming Messiah, what does this teach us about the character and the ministry of Jesus?

2. Consider the prophetic fulfilment of verse 9 which you see in Matthew 21:1 – 9 and John 12:12 – 16.

3. Given that Jerusalem has been overrun on a number of occasions since Zechariah's day do you think the promise of security for Jerusalem in verse 8 relates to a future millennial age or does it perhaps refer to the impregnability of the Christian church (see Matthew 16:18)?

CHAPTER 10

The restoration of Judah (1 – 5)

The prophet calls on the people to trust
God for the abundant harvest spoken of in
chapter 9. Back in Egypt the source of vital
water was the Nile. In Canaan God would
provide for His people through rain at the
appropriate times. The temptation to follow
the so-called fertility gods of Canaan had
often caused the Israelites to fall away from
worshipping God. The frequent episodes of
Baal (*"the rider on the clouds"*) worship had
troubled them for centuries. In verse 2
"idols" refers to *"teraphim"*. These are
images representing household gods or
images used for ancestral worship. It is the
term used for the items that were stolen by
Rachel from Laban (Genesis 31:34), that
were made by Micah for his personal
shrine (Judges 17:5) and which Michal
used to fool Saul's men (1 Samuel 19:13).
They were also used to ask the spirit world
for decisions (Ezekiel 21:21). In the day of
revival under King Josiah their use was
strongly condemned (2 Kings 23:24).

In verse 3 God condemns the shepherds
(leaders) who have not properly cared for
His flock. God will visit His people Himself
and strengthen them. Indeed, they will

become like a mighty war horse that carries Him into battle. God's people will not win victories because of their military prowess or tactics but because of the Lord's overpowering presence.

The restoration of Israel (6 – 12)

Verse 6 marks a transition from the transformation of Judah to the transformation of Israel (Joseph). The house of Joseph refers to the tribes from the northern kingdom who were taken into exile when their capital, Samaria, fell to the Assyrians in late eighth century BC. God now promises to save them and restore them to their former state *("they will be as though I had not rejected them"* - v 6*)*.

The restoration of Israel is based on God's compassion and His covenant. The link is made in verse 6. God will hear them because He is merciful and because He is, and has always remained, *"their"* God, He has not abandoned His covenant with them despite their disobedience.

The exiled Israelites who had been defeated, depressed and decimated will become mighty men who rejoice and are glad (7). God will gather and redeem them from the nations and they will see increase and prosperity once again. God will bring them back from Egypt and Assyria (10) and will plant them in Gilead which is between the Sea of Galilee and the Dead Sea, east of the Jordan and Lebanon which is to the north of Israel where some of the Israelites had lived prior to defeat by the Assyrians.

Verse 11 has echoes of the Israelites' deliverance from Egypt when they were led by Moses. Here, however, it is God Himself who is seen as passing through the seas of water and affliction. God destroys the pride and rule of those nations who had previously held His people captive.

Just as he promised to strengthen Judah (6) so now God makes the same promise to Israel (12). They will be enabled to walk in His Name.

There are a number of theories as to how and when this prophecy will or has been fulfilled. We may need to wrestle with whether this is referring to the scattered tribes of Israel, some of whom did return to the land, but few in number, or to a future return of the Diaspora, as some see since the creation of the state of Israel after World War 2. Alternatively, it may be a reference to God bringing in all nations into His family as the Christian Church fulfils His commission.

Questions to think about and discuss

1. How does this chapter help us understand what God most desires for His people?

2. What idols were tempting God's people?

3. As you reflect on Zechariah's message for God's people in this chapter what would you say is the brightest promise it contains?

4. What do you think is this chapter's most powerful image of a future day?

CHAPTER 11

Announcing judgement (1 – 3)

After the bright hope for the future announced in chapter 10 this section snaps the readers or hearers back into the present reality. These three verses all deal with judgement and disaster. They describe disasters in the natural realm (cedars, pine, oaks, pastures, lush thicket). Lebanon was well known for its cedar forests (e.g. Isaiah 14:8), a source of timber for the palace and temple in Jerusalem. In Ezekiel 31 cedars are used as a figure concerning the downfall of Assyria and Egypt. The cedars of Lebanon and oaks of Bashan symbolized the arrogance of humanity in Isaiah 2:12 – 17.

The destruction causes laments by the trees and the shepherds. Jeremiah uses remarkably similar vocabulary in 25:34 – 38, a section that includes prophecy of the destruction coming to Judah but also the subsequent destruction of Babylon. It is also similar to Isaiah 10 where the prophet speaks of God's judgment on Assyria and concludes by speaking of God's destruction of the thick forests of Lebanon.

Prophetic signs of the shepherd and the sheep (4 – 16)

This section contains prophetic signs using the familiar picture of shepherds and how they care and protect their flocks or, alternatively, misuse them and fail to protect them. The main lesson is that if people will not listen to good leaders they will suffer under numerous evil ones (the three shepherds v 8). The good shepherd described takes two staffs and names them *"favour"* and *"union"*. Ezekiel did something similar in 37:13-23 but, when he used two sticks, he brought them together as a symbol of the unity of Judah and Israel. *"Favour"* represents God's blessing. When this staff is broken it symbolises the breaking of a covenant made with all the nations. *"Union"* is a Hebrew word related to the giving of an item as a pledge and is also related to the distribution of the Promised Land to the Israelite tribes (see Joshua 17:5,14. 19:9 & Ezekiel 47:13). When this staff is broken it symbolized the breaking of the bond between Israel and Judah.

We see here an incident regarding the paying of wages to the shepherd (v12 ff). The amount weighed out was 30 pieces of silver. This was the price of a slave that has been injured (see Exodus 21:32). This comparatively low amount indicates disapproval of the shepherd's efforts. The silver is then rejected and the coins thrown to the potter or smelter in the Temple (*"house of the Lord"*). We may see here a prophecy of the story of Judas' betrayal of Jesus (see Matthew 26:15).

In verses 15 and 16 we have another shepherd who will not only fail to care for his flock but will misuse them and use them for food. He is described as a *"foolish"* shepherd. In the Bible a *"fool"* is often seen as someone who is morally corrupt (Psalm 107:17), who has no fear of the Lord (Proverbs 1:17) or who refuses to make amends for their sin (Proverbs 14:9).

Judgement on a leader (17)

The final verse of the chapter is a pronouncement of woe against a leader or a worthless shepherd. *"Worthless"* is usually used as a term to describe idols and false prophets (see 10:10 and Jeremiah 14:14). The judgement will be severe with both right eye and arm affected. The only other *"sword"* judgment in the Old Testament is found in Jeremiah 50:35 -38 where the prophet attacks the

Babylonians for their idolatry and false prophecy. This perhaps suggests that Zechariah is announcing that the idolatrous shepherds of his day will be judged by the sword in the same way that the idolatrous Babylonians with their false prophets were judged at the beginning of the Persian rule.

Questions to think about and discuss

1. Look over verses 4 – 17. How would you explain the meaning and significance of what Zechariah does here?

2. In what ways, if any, is this book meeting your personal needs for perseverance and encouragement?

CHAPTER 12

The coming deliverance of Judah

This chapter is the first of the final oracles of Zechariah. In chapters 12 to 14 we find presented God's plan to both cleanse His people and defeat the opposing nations in a future day.

Chapter 12 (and continued to 13:6) is an oracle from God that outlines His comprehensive plan for the renewal of His people. He will make Jerusalem an impenetrable fortress against the surrounding nations. He will also use Judah to strike at those foreign forces before He transforms Jerusalem and His Davidic king into a mighty army. This move of God is only the first step in His plan for His people. He promises His people that He will work amongst them to:

- produce repentance in their hearts and minds
- provide cleansing for their sin
- remove idolatry from their midst
- remove false prophecy from the land

It seems clear that the political and religious situation in Jerusalem is not as God desires for His people.

There is mention of Shimei's Levitical line rather than Zadok's which may imply that God was displeased with that branch which had pre-eminence in Zerubbabel's time as Governor.

The repeated use of the phrase *"on that day"* throughout this section begs the big question - when will all this happen?

Introducing the God of the Oracle (1)

The description of God is as the one *"who stretches out the heavens, who lays the foundation of the earth..."*. This brings into focus the global dimension of God's dominion and reminds us of similar descriptions found in Psalms (i.e. Psalm 18:47-48), Job (5:9 -16), Amos (4:13) and Isaiah (40:22).

God is described as the Creator of all things including the formation of the spirit of humanity. Having established the power and right of God the oracle will proceed to proclaim what God will do in the future.

Victory for Jerusalem and Judah (2 – 9)

The prophecy describes a siege of Jerusalem by opposing forces consisting of all the surrounding people, all the nations of the earth. This is truly a force of global proportions. The opposing forces will be defeated but before this the leaders of Judah remind themselves that their strength comes from God (5).

In verse 6 God uses the leaders to bring victory and then in the second phase of battle God uses Jerusalem and the house of David as a fighting force. Some think that this is a prediction concerning Armageddon, the last major battle of history (referred to in Revelation 16:16 and 19:19). Others see this in a figurative sense, referring to the church, which is constantly besieged by enemies but never completely overthrown.

Jerusalem is described as a cup of drunkenness that sends the nations reeling (2) and an immovable rock that injures all who try to move it (3). In verse 4 God will strike the enemy cavalry with blindness, madness and confusion (see Deuteronomy 28:28).

Finally, in verse 6, God says He will make the Governors like fire pans and fiery torches that will utterly destroy their enemies but leave Jerusalem unscathed.

Mourning for the pierced One (10 – 14)

This section begins with a promise from God that He would pour out a spirit of grace and supplication on the people of

Jerusalem. Having promised external salvation from their enemies in the previous verses, now God promises an internal renewal of the nation.

God's pouring out of His Spirit is a declaration of His placing His unique and manifest presence upon His people. The idea of God pouring our His Spirit is also seen in Ezekiel 39:29 and Joel 2:28-29. The Spirit of *"grace and supplication"* highlight two aspects of the ministry of the Holy Spirit: granting His people favour with Himself through renewed relationship and bringing them to return to Him in repentance.

The remainder of this section describes the impact of God's Spirit on the community. Most of the imagery is drawn from the context of mourning for the dead. They are mourning someone they have *"pierced"*. The questions are whose death are they mourning and when will this happen?

In verse 10 the mourning is intense. It is described as the kind of mourning experienced at the death of a first born and only son. The death of such a one would be devastating as he would have represented the hope of the continuance of the family.

The details in verse 11 are more confusing. Some see in it an allusion to the death of King Josiah in the plain of Megiddo (2 Chronicles 35:25). *Hadad Rimmon* may be an unidentified place in the valley of Megiddo. An alternative view is that the words refer to either Baal or a Semitic storm God called Hadad. *"Hadad the Thunderer"* is mentioned in the Babylonian *"Epic of Gilgamesh"* and the mourning rites associated with his worship (see 1 Kings 18, 1 Kings 15:18, 2 Kings 5:18).

In verses 12 to 14 we have a list of all those who are mourning the One pierced. Every family will mourn. There is mention of David (royal), Nathan (prophetic), Levi (priestly) and Shimei (wisdom). They could also be described as the royal (David & Nathan) and priestly (Levi & Shimei) lines.

The description of the One pierced reminds many of the picture of the Suffering Servant found in Isaiah 53. This is then seen as a picture of Jesus and His crucifixion. In John 19:37 the writer directly applies the description in Zechariah to the crucifixion. However, we should perhaps note that in Isaiah the piercing leads to salvation whereas here it leads to people simply mourning with no hint of salvation.

Questions to think about and discuss

1. In your own words, what would you say God wants us to understand most about Himself from verse 1?

2. What words or phrases in this chapter tell us most about God's purpose and plan for His people?

3. How was the meaning of verse 10 regarded by the apostle John in John 19:34 – 37?

CHAPTER 13

Idolatry cut off and false prophets destroyed (1 – 6)

Continuing from chapter 12 the prophecy continues concerning the future day when God would destroy Judah's enemies. Echoing the promise in 12:10 of the pouring out of a spirit of grace and supplication, in 13:1 we have another expression of refreshment and also of cleansing. This time it is a picture of a fountain being opened up. This fountain we are told would deal with sin and uncleanness.

At the same time God would also deal with idols, false prophets and unclean spirits. During this time, it seems that any prophecy uttered would be considered to be false. This may indicate that as God has spoken His final word with the coming of Jesus the Messiah there is no longer any need for prophecy.

The actions of the parents seen in verse 3 is in accordance with Deuteronomy 13 where verse 5 commands that there should be no toleration of false prophecy connected with idolatry. There is also an echo of the end of chapter 12 where God is pierced, here the false prophet will be *"thrust through"* (NKJV).

In verses 4 and 5 those who had previously prophesied will try to cover this up by claiming to have other vocations and by not wearing the prophet's robe. The choice of profession (farmer) may remind us that Amos had been called by God from being a herdsman. Now the false prophets are claiming they always were farmers. We are also reminded of Elijah's cloak and coarse belt being a sign of his authority (1 Kings 19:13, 2 Kings 1:8).

The mention in verse 6 of wounds is probably a reference to the pagan practices of cutting the body in their rituals.

The Shepherd Saviour (7 – 9)

The sword is a regular metaphor in the prophetic books for death and judgment (Isaiah 34:5 – 6, Ezekiel 5:1). In Jeremiah 47:6 the sword, as a personification, is spoken to directly by humans and in Ezekiel 21:16 (as here in verse 7) the sword is spoken to by God. The message is that the shepherd is doomed because the sword is told to strike the shepherd.

The shepherd is referred to as *"My shepherd"* and *"My companion"* by God. Shepherd is sometimes used to refer to political and religious leaders. In Isaiah 44:28 it refers to Cyrus, whom God raised up to accomplish His purposes. In Ezekiel 34:8 the reference is an attack on the leadership of his day.

The result of the attack on the shepherd is that the flock is scattered. The scattering leaves the *"little ones"* vulnerable to being attacked. Perhaps surprisingly the attack comes from God who turns His hand against them. God will discipline His flock in order to purify them. Following the purification of His people the covenant relationship between them and God is restored. The people will now seek Him and God will respond to them by calling them again *"His people"*. These declarations echo a number of covenantal declarations throughout the history of Israel, see also Jeremiah 24:7, Ezekiel 11:20, Hosea 1:9.

Questions to think about and discuss

1. Which of the prophecies in this chapter would you say point most directly to Jesus?

2. Look at the prophecy in verse 7 and compare it to how Jesus used this passage in Matthew 26:31 – 35 and Mark 14:27 – 31.

3. Verse 1 speaks of a cleansing for sin that is available. Do we behave as if the comment *"Nothing is too bad or too big to be forgiven"* is really true?

CHAPTER 14

Judgement on Jerusalem (1 – 2)

In Scripture the *"day of the Lord"* is usually a reference to the end times. The nature of the language in this chapter, as in Revelation, is apocalyptic (highly symbolic, prophetic). This makes it difficult to decide what is due to take place literally and what is symbolic, happening only in type or in the spiritual realm.

In the first two verses there is described a judgement on Jerusalem and its inhabitants. God would allow the surrounding nations to besiege and take the city. The city would be plundered, the women ravished and half of the population would be taken into captivity. Only a remnant of the population would remain in the city.

The appearance of God (3 – 5)

Having brought disaster upon Jerusalem now God marches out against its enemies. The appearance of God (a theophany) is upon the Mount of Olives. God's appearances are often on mountains in the Old Testament (Mount Sinai, Mount Zion). The abandonment and then return by God may perhaps be reminiscent of Ezekiel's vision found in 11:23 and 43:1-5. There,

Ezekiel links God's abandonment of His people to the idolatrous behaviour of his generation (Ezekiel 8:5 – 18), a connection that may explain the reference to *"east of Jerusalem",* which was the site of much idolatry throughout the history of Israel (1 Kings 11:7, 2 Kings 23:23).

When God appears, there is a huge earthquake that transforms the geography around Jerusalem. There is a newly created valley that can be used by those left behind in Jerusalem as an escape route prior to the final battle and also as a path for the triumphal return of God to His seat of rule. The reference to the *"holy ones"* who will accompany God is a difficult phrase to determine. Some see it as meaning that God will be accompanied by angels when He comes to do battle, others see it as referring to people who will return with Him drawn from amongst the remnant who had been previously purified by God.

God assumes His rule and transforms the cosmos (6 – 11)

God's appearance affects the natural order with the cycle of day and night, light and dark being transformed. Perhaps here is seen a reversal of the account of creation found in Genesis chapter 1.

Jerusalem becomes a source of *"living water"* for both east and west. *"Living waters"* is a description for fresh water originating in a well or spring. We may perhaps spiritualise it as being a flow of spiritual life (see John 7:38).

Verse 9 makes the declaration of God's rulership over all the Earth. The declaration that *"the Lord is one and His name is one"* may remind us of the *Shema* of Deuteronomy 6:4-5.

Verse 10 sees a further transformation of the land as the land drops to form a plain between Geba and Rimmon. Jerusalem will now tower over the surrounding area. The spacious city will be filled with inhabitants who will enjoy security. God's presence in the city produces unprecedented security both from the internal judgement of a holy God and from external threats from foreign invasion.

Defeating the nations (12 – 15)

God has established His base in Jerusalem and now strikes His opponents with an unprecedented plague. The description in verse 12 of what will happen to these enemies may be an ancient description of the terrible effects of modern warfare. The plague will produce overwhelming panic among the armies of the nations. In the confusion they will engage in hand-to-hand combat (see also Judges 7:22). The plague will affect not only the people but also the animals used in their warfare. The defeat of God's enemies is confirmed by the collection of much plunder including gold, silver and clothing.

The nations worship the King (16 – 21)

Following the defeat of the nations those who remain among them will now begin to make annual pilgrimages to Jerusalem to honour God. Specific mention is made of the Feast of Tabernacles. This feast is a celebration of God as Creator and Redeemer, the One who provides the harvest (Deuteronomy 16:13-17) and who also rescued His people from Egypt (Leviticus 23:39 – 43). Anyone who does not participate will find they have no rain for their crops. Amongst these Egypt is particularly mentioned.

From that time even common utensils will share the status of the sacred bowls at the altar. The term *"holiness unto the Lord"* was previously only inscribed on the head plate of the High Priest (see Exodus 28:36-38). Now its use would be extended. Previously horses were ritually unclean animals (see Leviticus 11:1-8), now in the new Jerusalem they too will be made clean.

As the commonest of utensils will now be seen as holy there will be no further need for merchants in the Temple precincts. The term *"Canaanite"* in verse 21 is one used for the inhabitants of the land of Israel prior to their conquest of the Promised Land. It can also denote the merchants who bought and sold goods (see Isaiah 23:8 and Proverbs 31:24).

This final oracle brings the book to a climactic close. Its cosmic vision of God's kingship is powerful. The picture of the divine warrior whose very presence can shake the cosmos is one that can stir our hearts for this is OUR GOD. God's people will be cleansed and His and our enemies will be defeated. The nations will bow before Him and acknowledge Him for who He is, the everlasting King of kings and Lord of lords. To a nation like Judah who had been subjugated by the superpowers of their day this was a word of hope and comfort. It is still so today for us.

Questions to think about and discuss

1. Chapter 14 has been called the key to the book of Zechariah. What does this chapter include that could make it this significant?

2. What are the most important things this chapter communicates about God's character and personality?

3. What are the most important things this chapter communicates about God's purposes and plans for His people?

MALACHI

MALACHI

Who was the author?

Nothing is known about the prophet Malachi apart from this book. We are not even sure that Malachi was the name of the prophet. The word means *"My Messenger"* and it is possible that the first verse should be translated *"The burden of the word of the LORD to Israel by My Messenger."* In any case, Malachi's name identifying him as a messenger of God highlights one of the major themes of the book. Malachi prophesies that God would send a *"messenger".* This can be taken in at least two ways. Firstly, it could be seen as a prophecy of the coming of John the Baptist. Secondly, it may be seen as a prophecy of the coming of Jesus, *"the Messenger of the covenant".* (3:1).

In 2:7 the role of a priest is described as *"messenger of the LORD of hosts."* Based on that description, a priest-prophet in the Temple might have used the designation *"My Messenger"* for himself. Because of the writer's apparent concern with the priesthood, it may be argued that the author of the book was a priest to whom God also gave a prophetic message.

From the content of the book it is likely that the writer was a contemporary of Nehemiah. Some scholars believe the book was actually written by Ezra using the pseudonym of Mal'aki. Whoever the author was, Malachi is the last of the twelve Minor Prophets, the final inspired writer of Scripture until the New Testament.

When was the book written?

There is wide agreement that the Book of Malachi was written during the last half of the fifth century BC. Some commentators pinpoint the date between 420 and 415 BC. This would place the Book of Malachi about one hundred years after the ministries of Haggai and Zechariah. There are numerous similarities in the book to the concerns facing Nehemiah, who was the governor in Judah around 440 BC.

These include:

- marriages with foreign women (Nehemiah 13:23–27)

- not paying tithes (Nehemiah 13:10–14)

- neglecting the Sabbath (Nehemiah 13:15–22)

- a corrupt priesthood (Nehemiah 13:7–9)

- injustice (Nehemiah 5:1–13).

Historical setting of the book

After the great turmoil of the wars of the Assyrians, Babylonians and the Medes and Persians, a period of comparative peace came to Israel's part of the ancient world. The books of the pre-exilic prophets had been formed in the crucible of international wars and catastrophes. But under Persian rule the people of God were permitted to return to their land in peace. For a time, the constant threat of international conflict did not loom over their heads. The Persians collected taxes but other than this they were content to leave the Jewish people undisturbed. However, economic shortages were still common during this period.

Main themes in the book

The history of the Jewish people is a story of a recurring pattern of captivity, exodus and restoration into which Malachi also falls. There are two captivities in the Old Testament story and two accounts of an exodus of the Jewish people from captivity. The first captivity and the great Exodus is Israel's experience with Egypt at the beginning of Israel's history; the second is Israel's experience with Babylon.

In the account of the first Exodus Moses and Aaron occupy themselves to a significant degree with the issue of the proper worship of the living God, which was centred on the Tabernacle. A significant portion of the Book of Exodus, the whole of Leviticus, and parts of Numbers and Deuteronomy provide guidance for worship at the Tabernacle. The central aim of the Exodus was the creation of the people of God as a worshipping community (see Exodus 5:1).

Two of the books of the second exodus, the return of God's people from Babylon, concern themselves with the proper worship of God. These two books, Haggai and Malachi, focus on worship in the rebuilt temple. Haggai called the people to rebuild the temple in Jerusalem in 520 BC. In a sense his book parallels the Book of Exodus in which God gave instructions for the construction of the Tabernacle.

Malachi parallels the Book of Leviticus in that both are concerned with how the people and the priests should act in the Temple. However, there are significant differences. Leviticus emphasizes what the people should do, what offerings they should bring and what calendar they should keep in their worship of God.

Malachi's emphasis is on the *attitude* of those who bring their worship to God. In Leviticus we read about how to worship God; in Malachi, the focus is on the heart of those who worship.

It is apparent that the priests of Malachi's time were indifferent to the rules of worship (1:6–14) and the people themselves had become apathetic about their offerings to God (3:6–12). Where did this neglectful attitude come from? In a critical introductory verse, God said to the people, *"I have loved you."* The response of the people was, *"In what way have You loved us?"* (1:2). The people's suspicion about the motives of God toward them resulted in their half-hearted response to Him. Their apathy toward God was also reflected in their relations with other people, especially their spouses. It had become common at this time for men to divorce their wives, often due to trivial matters. Such men ignored the fact that the Lord was a witness to their marriages. As a result, God ignored their offerings. The prophecy of Malachi is God's response to this *"loveless"* situation.

OUTLINE

The Lord's love for Israel

1:1 – 5

The failure of the priests

1:6 – 2:9

The unfaithfulness of God's people
2:10 – 16

The coming day of judgement

2:17 – 3:5

The blessing in giving

3:6 – 12

The destiny of the righteous and wicked
3:13 – 4:3

Final words of exhortation and promise

4:4 – 6

Overview of the book

Malachi is about the error of forgetting the love of God. When people forget God's love, it affects their attitudes, home and worship. With God's love and loyalty in doubt, sacred commitments no longer remain sacred. God sent His prophetic messenger, Malachi, to rouse the people from their spiritual stupor and to encourage them to return to the living God. The book of Malachi reveals a people who question the reality of their sin and the faithfulness of God. They are a thoroughly heart-hardened people.

The book ends on a poignant note with a confrontation between a disappointed God and a disappointed people. In a sense, Malachi shows that the Old Testament comes to a chasm, with the bickering voices of the people on one side and the stern warnings of God on the other. Only the Lord Himself could provide a way out of this impasse. Malachi looks forward to this deliverance. He speaks of the person (messenger) who would prepare the way for the Messiah. The promised Messiah was the only One who could bridge the widening chasm between the people and their God.

Key verses

3:1 – the prophecy of the coming of John the Baptist preparing the way for the Messiah

3:6 – the unchanging God

3:8 -10 – do not neglect giving tithes and offerings

4:1 – 3 – prophecy of the Day of Judgement

The message for us today

- The need for genuine worship and service

- Be prepared for the return of Jesus

- True repentance prepares the way for reform and Holy Spirit inspired revival

- God and His love do not change

- God refines those He loves

- Leaders in the church should live in such a way that God is given honour and glory

Questions to think about and discuss

1. Before beginning a closer look at Malachi, how would you summarize what you already know about the book?

2. If you are already familiar with this book which passages are your favourite parts of it?

3. Does it concern you that we do not really know anything about Malachi or even know for certain when he wrote the book?

CHAPTER ONE

Israel is God's beloved (1 – 5)

Malachi, the last of the 12 Minor writing
Prophets and the last canonical book of the
Old Testament, begins in a straightforward
way. It simply tells us what the book
contains, a prophecy. What that prophecy
contains, the word of the Lord. Who it is
was intended for, the people of Israel.
Finally, who brought the prophecy to the
people, Malachi.

We do not know who Malachi was, his
name simply means *"messenger"* or
"messenger of the Lord". Whoever he was
he was direct in his approach and had a no
nonsense approach to telling God's people
where they were going wrong.

The message came following the return
from the Babylonian exile. Many of the
issues raised by the prophet were those
that both Ezra and Nehemiah contended
with. It is possible that either they
responded to his ministry or he prophesied
later, when there was a reoccurrence of the
problems. In the KJV the first line is
translated as *"the burden of the word of the*

Lord". Malachi was going to unburden the heart of God towards His people.

The style of the prophecy is sometimes in the form of a question and answer session between God and the Israelites. The first statement that God makes and which the people question is *"I have loved you"*. The people want God to show and prove how He has loved them. He refers them to the choice he made to bless Jacob and his descendants rather than his brother Esau and his descendants. His choice of Jacob's descendants (the Israelites) was a permanent choice. Esau's descendants, spoken of as Edom and Edomites, would always be opposed to the Israelites and God would be opposed to them. It is through the Israelites that God's Messiah would come. Since He knew the future of the descendants of both sons of Isaac, He had chosen Jacob who would produce a better heritage for a nation through whom the blessing promised to Abraham would come (see Genesis 12:1-3). Esau wasted his birthright because he did not value it, (see Genesis 25:29-34).

Throughout the struggles of Israel during the years of their captivity, the Edomites demonstrated unacceptable behaviour (see

Lamentations 4:21, 22, Psalm 137:7, Ezekiel 25:12.) Although the Edomites might try to reclaim their territory and re-establish their identity, God would work against every effort they made in order to become a nation. Why? Simply because of their wicked behaviour towards the Israelites. Edom would never be permitted to become a nation; this was God's judgement against the Edomites for their wickedness.

We should note that although Edom would never again exist as a nation, the Idumeans, Edomites, as a people would live in the southern part of Palestine and from them would, eventually, rise the family of the Herods.

The danger of polluted offerings (6 – 10)

In these verses God accuses the Israelites of disrespecting Him as their Father and their Master. The question arises as to how they have done this. The answer is that because God was the Father of Israel (see Exodus 4:22 – 23) He deserved the honour that was due to a father. God created the nation of Israel by bringing it out of Egyptian captivity. If anyone deserved to be honoured by them, it was God. He was both the Father and Creator of the nation of Israel.

Not only was God their Father, He was also their Master and Israel was the servant. Once again, they were not obedient to God as their Master. Since God was their Creator, then He should have been honoured. If He was their Master, then He should have been obeyed.

How had they shown contempt for God? The religious leaders showed disrespect for God as their Creator and Master by not obeying the laws concerning the offerings at the altar. In other words, they totally disregarded God's laws, and by doing this, showed no respect for God as their Master.

God says to them that they have shown no respect because *"the food you offer on my altar is defiled"*. This was the altar where animals were sacrificed in accordance with the Law. By allowing the people to bring blemished animals as their sacrifices to the Lord, the priests were showing disrespect to God by violating the laws concerning sacrifices. They were offering blind and blemished animals to be sacrificed on the altar. According to the Law, only the best of the animals was to be offered as sacrifices to the Lord.

The people brought their offerings for sacrifice but it was the responsibility of the priests to check to see if an animal had any blemishes or defects. If they did, the animal should be rejected. Leviticus chapters 1 to 7 gives the most detailed description of Israel's sacrificial system. The system included five types of sacrifices. The sacrifices and offerings that were brought by the people were to be the physical expression of their inward devotion.

The five types of sacrifice were:

1. Burnt offering
2. Grain offering
3. Peace offering
4. Sin offering
5. Guilt offering

These five offerings composed the basic sacrificial system of Israel. The sacrificial system taught the necessity of dealing with sin and, at the same time, demonstrated that God had provided a way for dealing with sin.

Malachi rebukes the people for offering lame and even sick animals to God instead of their best. Effectively, the people were defiling the altar and despising God. God asks them, would their governor accept these offerings? The obvious answer is no! God goes on to warn them of the consequences if they do not change their attitude towards Him. He says that it would be better to close the Temple and not to offer the sacrifice than to offer anything which is contrary to the Law of God.

God will be feared among the nations (11 – 14)

God then declares that He does not depend solely on Israel for praise and glory. Even at this time God was receiving praise and worship from others who were not of Israel. There were already some Gentiles who had converted to the faith of Israel. Since the Israelites had been scattered throughout the nations during the captivities, then we can safely assume that some of them did their work in converting Gentiles to the faith of Abraham. The passage can also be seen as a Messianic prophecy of a time when the glory of God would be revealed to the whole world.

Through their violation of God's laws concerning sacrifice, they were demonstrating their belief that the Law of God was a heavy or intolerable burden to bear (see also 1 John 5:3.). What they were offering displayed the fact that they were behaving falsely towards God. They gave God the leftovers and what they themselves rejected. In doing this they displayed their lack of reverence for God. God responded by pronouncing a curse on those who behaved like this. The word that is translated as *"cursed"* in Hebrew is *'arar'* and it means to execrate, to loathe. In other words, God loathed anyone who offered unacceptable sacrifices to Him.

In considering this passage we should perhaps remember that we too are called to be examples to those around us. If people do not see us worshipping and serving God with a proper attitude or if Bible study, prayer and witnessing is not important to us, then they will not think it is important to them either. We can also have a similar attitude towards worship. We may come to worship services late. We may come to worship services to receive instead of giving. We may just mime the words of the hymns we sing. We may not really listen to what is being said or preached. We may just come and go through a ritual of worship! Malachi's words have a solemn message to contemporary Christians as well as to the people of his own time.

Questions to think about and discuss

1. What reasons today do people put forward for doubting the sovereignty of God in the world?

2. It is clear from Malachi that God chose Israel for His own purposes despite their failings. How encouraging is this to you if you believe that God has also chosen you?

3. How easy would it be for someone in a local church to stand up and question whether the church was being obedient to God?

CHAPTER TWO

A corrupt priesthood (1 – 9)

When God instituted the priesthood among the Israelites, He promised them the blessing of the support of the people if they carried out their duties according to His Law. When the people brought sacrifices to the altar, the priests had the privilege of taking some of the offering for their own use. The Levites, as priests, did not receive any land when the Israelites entered the Promised Land. They were chosen to serve God in the temple and the other tribes of Israel were to take care of their needs (see Numbers 18:21,24,31 and Numbers 18:25-26,28).

In Malachi's time the priests were not carrying out their duties faithfully. If they continued in their injustice and indifference, God would command a curse upon them which means that the priests would lose the support of the people. When God says, *"I will curse your blessings"*, He is speaking about the benefits that they enjoyed because they served in the Temple (Nehemiah 18:8-19).

In fact, because of their insincere service it seems that *"the curse"* had already begun. The poverty-stricken people of Jerusalem either could not bring sacrifices to the altar or the sacrifices that they brought were blemished. Consequently, God rebukes them. God says that He will *"rebuke"* their descendants. This could possibly mean that the descendants of the priests would be removed from being priests. The warning from God in verse 3 is very graphic. The existing priests would be removed in the same way that the refuse of the offerings was taken out of the city.

The covenant between God and the Levites is not specifically mentioned in the Old Testament, other than the fact that Levi was in a mutual covenant relationship with God as a part of the entire Israelite family (Deuteronomy 33:8-11). In God's covenant with Israel, the Levites were:

- given an intercessory relationship with the people as ministers to God on behalf of the people

- to be the teachers of the Law

- to set an example of purity and obedience to the people

- to demonstrate in their lives the nature of the commandments of God

- to administer justice and be peacemakers among the people

- to be known for the truth that proceeded out of their mouths

The priests of Malachi's day had lost their way. It might have been because they had forgotten God's Law (see Hosea 4:6), and so they did not know what to do according to God's Law, or it might have been because they weren't interested in God's Law. Whatever the reason may have been, Malachi says they were still under the condemnation of God for not functioning as priests as they should.

In Malachi, the spiritual leaders led people away from God. Through their behaviour they became blind guides in the sense that they did not honour the commandments of God (compare to Mark 7:1-9).

The dangers of infidelity towards God (10- 12)

It is not only the priests (Levites) who have disobeyed God. In these verses we hear of the disobedience of the people of Judah. Despite many warnings from God and His prophets, men were marrying foreign women who were worshippers of other gods. By doing this they were destroying the identity of God's people among the nations. In other words, they were marrying themselves out of existence as Jews. God had established a covenant with Israel but their integration with the local people through marriage to foreign women violated the conditions of the covenant (see Deuteronomy 7:3-4). As a result of this, Malachi warns that God would cut off the males of the household who disrespected the covenant relationship between God and Israel through marrying foreign women. With the men being cut off from the household, there would be no one who could bring the offering to the Lord.

False tears of a false people (13- 16)

With the offering of sacrifices came the common practice of mourning for sin. In an effort to make their sacrifices more acceptable to God, people would pour out many tears and wail. However, we know that God desires obedience in all areas of our lives. Malachi says that they needed to change their behaviour, not pour out more ceremonial or emotional tears.

How were they disobeying God?

1. They were marrying foreign women.

2. They were abandoning their Jewish wives in order to marry the foreign women.

The older men were putting away the wives that they had married when they were young in order to marry younger, more beautiful wives in their older age. In other words, they had forgotten and broken the marriage covenant with their wives. When they married another, he or she comes into a covenant relationship with his or her partner. It is a covenant that is made in the eyes of God, and so it is honoured by God (see Genesis 31:50, Proverbs 2:16-17). When someone puts away his or her spouse, he or she has broken the marriage covenant.

In verse 15 we are told that spouses belong to one another *"body and spirit'*. This refers to the fact that when two people are joined together in marriage, they become one in order to produce children to the glory of God. Parents who demonstrate godliness in their lives may raise children who will continue their spiritual heritage (see Ephesians 5:22-6:4). This is not always the case, sometimes children will grow up and do their own thing and go their own way, no matter how godly their parents are or how great the example they have been .

It appears that the Jewish men were putting away the Jewish wives of their youth, so that they could marry foreign women. As a consequence of this, they were bringing the influence of idolatry again into Israel. There was a real danger that by doing this they could influence their children away from God.

Verse 16 mentions divorce. Moses gave instructions concerning the *"Certificate of Divorce"* (see Deuteronomy 24:1-9). The provision of the *"Certificate of Divorce"* was given to bring the Israelites into conformity to God's law concerning marriage. God's ideal was that one man should be married to one woman for life (see Matthew 5:31-32, Matthew 19:3-10, Mark 10:1-12). The Hebrew word for divorce is *"shalach"* which means to send away or put away. God hated the putting away of a first wife so that a man could marry another woman. The divorce referred to here was based on the desire a man had toward another woman other than the wife of his youth. In other words, divorcing was not the real issue, it was the way they in which they were divorcing. They were seemingly trading their old wives in for younger ones and divorcing their wives without the use of the *"Certificate of Divorce"*. In effect, it would be an illegal divorce. A woman could not marry anyone else unless she had this certificate and if she did marry without it, she would become an adulterer.

Wearying God (17)

This verse introduces us to those who had *"wearied"* God with their complaints. They said that God was looking after evil people but neglecting His own people (see Isaiah 1:14, Isaiah 43:24). The struggling Israelites looked to the nations from which they had come back from exile and wondered why those nations were prospering and yet they themselves were struggling to survive. Their struggles led them to doubt whether God was actually with them. They failed to look at their behaviour as being the cause of the cessation of God's blessing on them.

Questions to think about and discuss

1. What sins and failures does God highlight in this chapter? How might these be evident in today's church?

2. The priests of Malachi's day were failing and God takes them to task. How might God's words here impact the lives of ministers of the gospel in our days?

3. From this chapter how might you summarise God's expectations of His people and His ministers?

CHAPTER THREE

The coming Messenger (1 – 5)

God promises that He will deal with those who lived unrighteously and yet thought that they could still prosper. The time will come when He will stop that kind of thinking when He sends His messenger. This passage is quoted in reference to the coming of John the Baptist (Mark 1:2 – 3, Isaiah 40:3-5, Isaiah 52:7, Isaiah 57:14.)

As we have seen, the priests in Malachi's time showed partiality to the wealthy which is similar to the attitudes and actions of the priests of Jesus' time (Luke 16:14). This perhaps indicates that the coming of the Messenger would be in a time similar to that which Malachi was experiencing in his generation.

The second messenger who is spoken of here is a different messenger than the one who was promised at the beginning of the verse. This second one is the incarnate Lord Jesus, the Messenger of the new covenant. He is not only the Messenger but also the Mediator of the new covenant (Hebrews 12:24).

We should note that the judgement of God would firstly come to His people (His Temple) and He would cleanse His people from their sin. In other words, the Lord Himself would come to purify the priesthood. He is coming to execute judgement upon the unrighteous. The Lord would purify His people like a refiner's fire would purify metal and how a launderer would use soap to cleanse. A launderer was someone who bleached and cleansed clothes (see Revelation 7:14). When His people have been refined, they will bring acceptable offerings to God.

God will testify against a number of classes of people who do not fear Him and who behave in ways that are contrary to His commands. They include:

- sorcerers
- adulterers
- perjurers
- those who defraud workers of their wages
- those who oppress widows and orphans
- those who act unjustly towards foreigners

In God's kingdom and church there is no place for people like this.

The unchanging God (6 – 7)

Men may change in terms of their obedience to God but God does not change His commandments in order to comply with the behaviour of men. He also does not change regarding His promises (Hebrews 6:17 – 18). God still had a claim over the Jews as His people. Consequently, God did not cast away His people as He did the nations that surrounded them, including the nations that had taken them into captivity. God could have justly cast off His people because they broke the conditions of the covenant but, because He does not change, He maintained the covenant in order to preserve His people.

Returning to God through repentance is more than just a change of mind and a sorrow for sin. It is a change in behaviour, it is a return to obedience to the will of God (Matthew 3:8). True repentance will be demonstrated by a change in behaviour, actions speak louder than words.

Robbing God (8 – 12)

God now accuses His people of a specific way in which they were disobedient to Him. According to the Law, a tenth of the produce and livestock was to be given to God to provide the food for the Levites. This was commanded in Leviticus 27:30-32 and Numbers 18:21-24. It was confirmed in Nehemiah's time that the commandment remained in place (Nehemiah 10:32-39, Nehemiah 13:10-14). The people were robbing God in that they were not giving what was required by the Law. Because of their disobedience God says they are *"under a curse"*.

We may be reminded that during the days of Haggai, the land was suffering from drought because the people were being indifferent concerning the reconstruction of the Temple. A similar situation may have prevailed in Malachi's time because the people were being lax in bringing the required offerings. They were consuming the produce themselves, rather than bringing the tithe as their offering to the Temple for the priests.

The people were evidently holding back part of the tithe for themselves, believing that they needed it more than the priests. The situation may have been that only a few were offering their tithes, and so the support of the priests depended on the support of a few. Others were robbing God by not tithing at all. Malachi's message was that everyone must bring their tithe to the Temple in order that the priesthood could be supported (see Nehemiah 13:10-12, 1 Corinthians 9:14).

The grain offerings were to be stored in the Temple but God had *"held back the rain"* in order to bring about their repentance. If they were obedient in bringing their tithes, then God would bring them rain and hence the crops would grow.

Despite their poverty, Malachi says that they were to show their obedience to God's Law in respect to tithing. It was not the case that God would first bless them with rain for their crops, and then they would give out of their abundance. The lesson was that they should give out of their poverty and then God would send the abundance (see also Haggai 2:19, Zechariah 8:9-13, Luke 21:1-4).

The subsequent prosperity of the land would be the signal to the nations around them that God was blessing His people because of their obedience to His will.

We should remember that is a specific prophetic word to the Israelites of Malachi's time. We should take care not to assume that financial prosperity will follow our tithing today. God will bless His people for their obedience in all things and material prosperity is only one way in which God blesses them. In Malachi's day God prospered Israel in order to preserve the nation for the coming of the Saviour.

The people complain against God (13 – 15)

The people have become sceptical concerning the presence of God's help among them. They had been talking among themselves, speaking arrogantly about their circumstances and in their arrogance, they were actually murmuring against God. They had concluded that there was no benefit in being faithful to God because God was not bringing blessings into their lives.

They were mourning instead of rejoicing. The reason for this was that they had only kept up an outward appearance of obeying the ordinances of God but, inside, they were grumbling against God because He had not prospered them. At the same time, they saw the pride of the nations around them go unpunished by the Lord. They thought that if other nations can live with idolatry and still be wealthy, why then should we not also do so? Consequently, they refused to repent of their idolatry and grumbled about God's mistreatment of them.

God remembers those who love Him (16 – 18)

Those who feared the Lord are a different group of people from those who grumbled against God. This godly group listened to the words of Malachi. They understood that their situation was caused by their unrepentant behaviour. In obedience to God they turned from their wayward ways. Malachi confidently prophesies that they would be remembered by God in His book of remembrance.

God says that these people *"will be my treasured possession"*. God treasures those who serve Him. It is for this reason that the church of God's people is His unique possession (1 Peter 2:5-10). Not only is God's promise to preserve those who fear Him valid in this life, but also in the eternal life to come. Once the godly applied themselves to repentance and a change in their behaviour, they would be blessed by God.

Questions to think about and discuss

1. The call to repentance is not a popular message. Is there a case for omitting this requirement when we evangelise and instead concentrate on the attractive reasons for becoming a Christian? What do you think Malachi would say?

2. How have you experienced God's abundant love?

3. How easy is it to distinguish between righteous and ungodly people today? Should we be judging anyway?

CHAPTER FOUR

The Great Day of the Lord (1 – 3)

As we enter the final chapter, which is the final prophecy given to the Jews in the Old Testament, we need to keep in mind a couple of important things. The prophecy was to a people whom God had used since the days they were delivered from Egyptian captivity in order to preserve the promises made to their fathers, (Genesis 12:1-3). Earlier prophets had spoken of a Messiah who would come to Israel. In this final short prophecy we read again of the One who will come.

We believe that this is the last message the Jews heard from God for 400 years until John the Baptiser stood on the banks of the river Jordan and proclaimed *"repent, for the kingdom of God is at hand"* (Matthew 3:2).

When the Day comes when God intervenes finally the imagery given here is of a furnace. The unrighteous will be destroyed, consumed like stubble. The righteous, those who are obedient and faithful to God, will have a totally different experience. We are told that the *"Sun of*

Righteousness" will rise upon them and bring healing and joy. They also will trample the unrighteous underfoot. Who is the *"Sun of Righteousness"*? Jesus was the rising light who brought hope to those who feared God and were living at the time of His first coming (John 1:4-9, John 3:19-21, John 8:12). He will be so again when He returns at His Second Coming.

The final promise (4 – 6)

The statement to remember the Law of Moses should cause us to remember what Moses had told the Israelites. The encouragement here was that Israel will continue to remain under the statutes of the Old Testament Law in order that they might be preserved until the coming of the Messiah.

God says that *"He will send the prophet Elijah"*. This statement refers to John the Baptist (Matthew 11:14, Luke 1:17). It identifies the time of the historical fulfilment of this prophecy. John the Baptist, as the forerunner of the Messiah, operated in the power and spirit of Elijah. This coming of the Lord in the prophecy is a reference to the coming of the incarnate Son of God. His coming was a *"terrible day"* for those who rejected Him (John 12:48). There was a call from both John the Baptist and Jesus to repent (see verse 6).

There was a first fulfilment of the events of this prophecy in the 1st century with the coming of the messenger and forerunner of the Son of God, and the actual coming in the flesh of the Son of God (John 1:1-14). We might reflect on the destruction of Jerusalem in AD 70 when God brought national Israel to an end and the Jewish people were scattered from the Promised Land. Is that the fulfilment of the prophecy given in verse 6? Those who did not repent under the ministries of John the Baptist and Jesus were destroyed.

The second fulfilment of the prophecy will be the coming of Jesus at the end of time. This will not be a coming that is accompanied by a call for repentance. It will be a coming of finality, judgement and destruction (2 Thessalonians 1:6-9). It will be a coming to call God's people out of this world (1 Thessalonians 4:13-18).

It is sobering to think that after the unfolding revelation of God to Israel over many years His final words to them are the threat of a curse. Thankfully, we can contrast this with the final words of blessing from the book of Revelation, "***the grace of the Lord Jesus be with God's people. Amen.***"

Questions to think about and discuss

1. What similarities and differences can you find between the last chapters of the Old and New Testaments?

2. Malachi looks forward to a coming Day of the Lord. How would you answer someone who claimed that they knew the date of that Day?

3. Using a concordance write down all the Old Testament references you can find to the "Day of the Lord". How similar are they in their descriptions?

FINAL REFLECTION

We have now completed our studies of the three post-exilic prophets. Hopefully, you will have begun to appreciate the important place these books have in the canon of scripture.

Each of the prophets was called by God in a particular time and setting. Each called out to their fellow Israelites to obedience to following the Lord. In the midst of differing, troubled circumstances they faithfully delivered their messages. We do not know for certain how their messages were received. Sadly, we do know that after Malachi's message the prophetic word to the Israelites was silent for 400 years. In that time the religious life of the people varied in terms of obedience. Those who sought to preserve God's word amongst His people were few and far between.

Politically the region would be conquered by successive regimes. By the time that God began again to speak prophetically, through John the Baptist, Jerusalem and the Promised Land were under the control of the pagan Roman Empire. The Jewish religion was an allowed religion within the Empire and so there was little persecution. What we see of the religious life in Jesus' day indicates that there was a hunger for God in the hearts of some of the Jews. Others were satisfied with following the strict teaching of the scribes and the Pharisees and Sadducees. As Jesus would describe them there was an outward appearance of religion but no heart (see Matthew 23:13, 27). Perhaps the conditions in Jerusalem were not far different in Jesus' day than they had been in the days of Haggai, Zechariah and Malachi.

I would encourage you to continue to ponder the messages of these prophets. Their messages are timeless and, as the are the words of God, they are living and active.

If the Lord has spoken to you through this book please do get in touch, I would love to hear what God is saying in these days to you.

Be blessed in all you do for Him and for His glory alone.

David Chapman

Yaxley September 2020

davec1862@outlook.com

Other books available by David Chapman from Amazon in paperback and Kindle editions:

"The Faithfulness of God" – a daily devotional on God's faithfulness to His people and His promises

"The Supremacy of Jesus" – a pocket guide to Hebrews

"Gospel Truth in Practice" – a pocket guide to Ephesians

"Jesus Son of God Son of Man" – a pocket guide to Mark's Gospel

"For such time as this" – a pocket guide to Esther

"Hope in times of suffering" – a pocket guide to Peter's letters

Printed in Poland
by Amazon Fulfillment
Poland Sp. z o.o., Wrocław